a Quest
Among the
Bewildered

by

Wulf
Zendik

This writing was begun in Laurel Canyon—1957 and completed in Paris—1958. It is no more or less incoherent than I during that time.

Published by **Zendik Communal Arts**
370 Regan Jackson Rd.
Mill Spring, NC 28756
www.zendik.org
www.aquestamongthebewildered.com

To the whole crowd of hungry,
angry, hurting, defeated ones.
I go Don Quixote tower toppling.

Who am I? How can I say, what can I
tell you, tell myself — is there a title I
might apply? No, I'll use this book and
others — yes, I may write others — yes, I may
never write this one — yes, I may come alive
— this will let us know who I am. Let's say
the thing I do is light dark corners — I pick
up rotten logs in the dark corner of my mind
and look there — my hand shakes — my eye has
difficulty in focusing — yes I am frightened.
But wait, hand me the light, look at the
evil with things crawling over and through
each other — they die in the light — doesn't
evil always? My light is so dim, has almost
gone out many times — if you want to write to
me I think it would be nice.

— Wulf

Chapter headings by Wulf Zendik, reproduced from
drawings in the original manuscript

FLIPPING

Today they stopped the world
and I got off and it was lonely
and cold out there, and the world
spun on out into and through the
nothingness, and I knew
I was no colder or lonelier
than when I clung to its
face — such terror
and lust and
brutality
there
and,

yes,
stupidity — that
creeping, crawling
stupidity, the thing of lust and
greed oozing over the earth. And I didn't want to
go back, didn't want to leave my lone, impenetrable
isolation, my fortress of disdain. I remembered
their faces, their laughing and frozen faces — and
the fear — the wild rampant fear, and how each with
miraculous cunning and intricate craftsmanship
was building his little fences of the mind, little
fences of things known and understood, little
fences of things felt warm and comfortable with —
these portable, moveable fences, so cleverly
fabricated — they push in closer and closer,
surrounding the wild-fiendish-screaming *fear* — ever
closer, ever tighter around the little fear-room —
there — deep down, boiling inside the brain, the
unconscious — the unknown — like the fire in the pit
of a volcano — it sometimes finds a fissure — and
bursts and explodes, tearing through the fragile
walls of mind and soul — the pretty little woven
walls of dreams and fantasy disintegrate — and the
hot, toxic, molten, searing fear runs wild — wild
with long-sought victory — through the arteries, the
nerve-trails, the reason — and the man or woman or

1

child — yes child — becomes the thing, becomes the
omnipresent fear — and the head is beaten against
the wall, or the cock is always hard, or quietly
they set to work sharpening the kitchen knife and
lovingly and longingly gaze at the swan-like
movement of her beautiful neck — or they're locked
in a diminutive room, with the walls made soft —
a room built by society, where the walls are *not* of
dreams and fantasy — paranoia — schizophrenia —
psychosis — dementia praecox — what difference?
Fear — wild, loose, free fear.

  I know that as a boy, as a child, I accepted
nothing — everything was a Why to me. Why mommy,
why daddy, why teacher — bullshit teacher, don't lie
teacher, just tell me why!

  Has man progressed psychologically? In all of
recorded history — not that I can see. I remember
just a few short years ago another little impotent
psychopath destroyed a large chunk of earth and
souls. He stood and said to a group of psychopaths
as stupid but not so cunning as himself, "You are
supermen" — and they believed him and built iron-
doored ovens for baking Gypsy & Jew and cruel-
treaded tanks for smashing Poles and supersonic
rockets for disintegrating English... No don't
prattle to me of man's social progress! The same
thing can, and might, happen in America, North or
South — France — anywhere. People are people and
they all, no matter what the color or form of their
skin and eyes and hair are filled with the same
feelings of inadequacy, incompetency, longing for
security, hate of mother and father and other men
and women — full of beaten, distorted, defiled,
twisted instincts. I'm saying that in our
contemporary world people still judge others by the
color of their eye or skin, and this is a living
hell we are in where a person's thoughts and
actions are relatively inconsequential compared

2

with the color of eye or skin. Think... Could you have devised a more effective hell?

All right, granted no progress intellectually, psychologically or sociologically — but technologically? Ah, yes — technologically we live in a fairyland where what man can conceive with mind, he can do with hand. The depth of oceans, the deepest depths of earth and the limitless expanse of space will be his, and for what? New battlefields, new arenas for conquest with his new death toys — no matter how devastating against his environment, himself, his own kind or perhaps one day against newly-encountered beings of space. Is there an alternative to this dire prediction? Is there no hope for these two-legged mammals gone mad? And why? Why? Because there is no Why — not a real, introspective Why, no beautiful Why. No, not one in a thousand thoughts. A thousand thoughts of material gain and physical conquest and intellectual pride — and not one Why of motive and desire, not one thought on True mental or physical cause-and-effect. Not one irreverently free of the fads and trends of the day. No such Why — No such Whys.

If the technical scientist in his sterile white coat in his sterile white laboratory looking through the might of his microscope, would turn that looking-glass inside himself, apply that incredibly channeled intellect to self-whys... as you must and I must — perhaps he would see and feel his need and look out the windows — do they still have windows in laboratories? — and see the earth and sky and sun and grass and birds and trees all busy with living, and think of the good of a woman to be loved, of soft earth under his feet, of laying on the grass talking with a friend he loves.

If a little psychopath stood and said to him or you, "Come — come with me — we will conquer the world and kill men and rape women — together we

3

will do this because you are clever and I am cunning and together we can take and take and have our way and be masters and they our slaves and rape is better than love" — what would you say? I know — Yes, I know he is clever. Yes, his cunning is gripping your ego tight and he knows precisely where to grab — knows where you are vulnerable — that is his business, to know your place of vulnerability — and you *are* vulnerable, you know. I am — you are — and he knows — knows where.

A Why to him, or profoundly to yourself, will stop him, or her or whoever or whatever wants hold of your ego. A Why — a simple Why — why do we want to conquer the world, why do you want to kill and rape, why do you need me — why do I want to go with you? Why are your soul-shackling laws right and my pleasure instincts wrong? And when you question them, interrogate them with your simple, repeated, sincere, curious, wide-eyed Why — at first the answer comes full with rhetoric, ostentatious, high-sounding... But Why — Why — Why — you gently pry at them, or hammer violently at them — but always the sincere Why. Little by little, sometimes slowly, sometimes quickly, they begin to deteriorate before your eyes — because they cannot answer — they have no truth — only greed to conquer and possess — and soon the evil stench of their disintegrating will fills the air and their hands fall, empty of your ego — empty of your soul — and you are free to go or to stay, help them or leave them, but *free*... And all you said was Why.

No don't prattle to me of man's approach to saintliness. Don't tell me that we've come a long way. Don't stand there defending Christianity, Judaism or any of them. Don't tell me that anything tried has ever worked. Don't tell me of man's spirit: Don't tell me of *his* ascent from protective night

fires and black bone-littered caves... No! No, tell
me of the stench of Auschwitz and Belsen and
discussing baked Jew over your Sunday barbeque. No—
no tell me of the sear and scream of flame and
mute silt of flesh and sightless moan called
Hiroshima.

When the ex-general stood up on TV saying, "We
now have clean bombs," was he implying the Hiroshima
one was dirty?

If you're looking for a stereotypical form of
communication, there's an excellent chance you'll
establish stereotypical communication... If you
find my writing offensive, you'll also find me
offensive. So close the pages — we are not for each
other.

What I usually do when I feel very tense is
go for a long walk. But you know, sometimes I stand
in the middle of the street feeling everything
pressing in on me, and I can't even make myself
move. I know if I walk long enough, the anxiety
will dissipate some, even if only from sheer
fatigue. But I won't move — it's too weird. So then I
just go back in my pad and flip. The one thing I
know is that if I flip badly enough, I've got to
learn and that's the only time I can, you know,
when I'm flipping.

You know, every time a little child mixes his
intestines with spilt oil under the broad wheels of
a careening truck and its drunken driver; or a
cyclonic wind comes and blows away a city and a
thousand lives — someone inevitably stands and
utters these words... "It was God's Will." Who in
Eternity's name is this person named Will — this
fiendish Machiavellian who turns lovely days into

holocausts and sucks the life from our friends and
children? God, if this notorious one they call
"Will" belongs to you, push a button — flip a switch —
do something, because he's messing up.

Wulf, your sweet Love just died! Oh, but don't
suffer so, my boy, the pain will go in time — after
all, "It was God's Will," you know. I turn upon my
comforter — there is a roaring inside me. I taste a
vile foam on my lips. My insides are aflame. The
fire spurts from my eyes. With an insane blow, I
disintegrate this comforter. I scream pain at the
walls — they shake, crumble, the roof crashing down
pins me to the floor — a girder, piercing my body,
presses against my heart — it keeps trying to beat
against the cold steel... I hear the curious, poking
through the wreckage, and the knowing voice of an
old lady. "It was God's Will."

The thing is, it's so confusing to be
confused...

One of the few things of value man has
achieved through technological progress is vapor
trails.

Hate! I'm filled with it — I taste it in my
throat, blurs my vision — hands like ice — head
bursting from the pressure. Conversation? Book?
Cigarette? Coffee? Grass? Liquor? No, none of
these. What can calm me? Nothing. I'll explode,
disintegrate — this is the end. Rush outside.
Street strange under my feet — the sky, sun, trees,
all foreign, strangers to me. Lost.

Dear God, having a hell of a time, wish you
were here. See, I cry for God. God who, God why, God
where, God what. I was the sun, the sky, the God.
They're all one, I them — no more, no more... People,
love and be loved, feel of warm flesh under my
fingers, around my fingers, lost. Ah, to lose self,

submerge self in a sea of flesh, slow sink my Self
deep and deeper. Yes, dear girl, so great our need —
it is so, we are need, not cool, not crisp, not
brittle, not Intellectual. Ah, this Life of the
Intellect leaves us cool, brittle. Girl-woman, come,
yes, surround me — yes, articulate breasts pointing
to me, touch me — yes only in this is femininity —
only in this is maleness — man woman — woman man,
only together, all everything, total, nothing
else, summation. Isolation is neuter. I enter! You
become sun, moon, sky, earth — female. I too, I am in
counterpart.

Ah, yes I hate. What else? — aloneness hate,
isolative hate. Our need overpowering, drove us
apart. The greater the need, the more desperate its
statement, the more terrifying to the needed...
Run. Yes, go — yes, run. I state here, I state now,
forever, my need of you. When you run, wherever you
run, my need goes with you, torn from me. Yes, yes,
of course it pains, of course, it pains, of course,
it pains. And it burdens you — yes!

I might call this book "I Write I Feel."

As I write this I see two men, high on a
scaffold, gluing large sheets of printed paper to a
massive, crude slab of tin. They are working very
hard — this is serious business. Very, oh, very
important. They step back, light cigarettes. I see
their feeling of accomplishment — Good Show — Well
Done — Bravo! The sign says "Drink Glub Glub Beer,
it's non-fattening" or some shit like that. These
guys were talking of their women as they worked.
Yes, yes it's true, I heard them. You must believe
this. It's true. These men who put up beer signs,
men who design beer signs, men who own beer signs
have women — I swear it! And these women (their
genitals are female) play bridge, watch daytime TV,

go to the beauty salons, chatter, destroy their children, cook from cans, so these idiots can go on with their beer signs. It's all too funny, so funny... Then why am I crying? I have none, I who brought a single wild petal to my love — I found it alone in a field. They give new refrigerators and black lingerie. Who's to say I'm right, they're wrong? I'm to say! I sit here in my beat car, on a parking lot off Sunset Strip, watching fools do foolish things. In the night, high above L.A., I look out over the city that has consumed my life. And I say I'm right, you're wrong; with your TV antennas and your neat little lawns and your meaningless lives — I'm right, you're wrong. Ratios — percentages — odds — they're millions against me. Still, I know I'm right. But I'm crying...

They don't cry. I looked into the eyes of my remembered love. Though it's gone now, our yes, our here, our moment was a thing of beauty, of life. But them — I know them — their mating is a thing for their plans of tomorrow — a thing for bargaining, for building security. I see this, and, yes, I hate them and their passive carefully contrived relationships. I am not passive, I'm not a passive friend or lover... The men have gone and I look up at the sign again. There's a girl that looks like her and she's eyeing some square over a glass of beer. It's really very funny... So why am I crying?

If I don't shoot poppy-juice or suck high-smoke anymore — it's only because I know it doesn't work. If there was a way out I'd take it. There is none. I know strength is knowledge — nothing works, only truth, nothing else, from this no escape... ever. Not for me... or her... or you.

People are always saying to me, "Oh, well, you don't like anything anyway, so what can we expect?"

8

Is it true, really, don't I like anything? Well, no.
Here, in art, in poetry, I don't. Either I love, or I
hate. But not so in my lesser life. There are films,
books, all sorts and kinds and stuff and people
that I just... like. It's of no consequence one way
or the other, whether I see them today, tomorrow, or
ever. They're convenient, fill in the harsh cracks,
round off the sharp corners — and it's bad! Bad for
me... They keep me from my suffering, smother my
pain with their soft smiles, soft handshakes, soft
sexings — keep me from my lunacy, my lovely lonely
lunacy... Stay away from me, dear sweet idiots — I'll
never go insane with your softness surrounding me —
I want my insanity or my lucidity — my degradation
or my greatness — no passive middle road for me —
No — the bottomless pit of hell or the pinnacle of
heaven is mine... For me the shrieking screaming
terror of loneliness must live with me — inside me —
feeding on my gut and soul and heart till we are
one — my loneliness and me — till we have accepted
one another — come to terms — joined as friends — till
I am the thing and the thing is me — loneliness. Yes,
we are one, and the shrieking and the screaming
will subside — and the waves of terror will crash no
more and it is calm and I am calm — and I love — yes,
love my aloneness — for united with Self — the final
Realization of Self, of mySelf, this Self, that Self,
my schized Selves, all of them, of Us, and yes we
are the peace of the ages — we are the Truth of all
living things. The Truth: *we are alone.* Now there is
nothing to fight, to beat against with the mind.
Life is — Truth is — Death is — alone — each alone —
aloneness is — yes is — in birth — in life in death —
love and hate — passion and sympathy... aloneness is.

You'll question this scream out of despair
with your trite little minds — you'll question the
inevitability of aloneness, this anomalous concept
of aloneness with your struggling brain? You'll

question this statement, this factual statement
of my Life, of all Life — of all Nature, this
irrevocable conclusion with your infinitesimal
mind? Yes... And yes, so will *I*. And I could love
you for this. For within my soaring comprehension,
we are Gods and earth our heaven — supreme we are —
and glorious — and we would question and question
till our question becomes a question and still we do
not fall to our knees slobber-wailing before a self-
conceived pagan deity for an Answer, because to the
intellectual coward even a bizarre myth is more
bearable than the lonely empty unknown. No! We
would stand alone — because aloneness is perhaps the
last Truth we will know — but it is True — and no
fantasy can erase or change this thing...

And now my goodbye to your unlived faces and
yestertimes' warmed-over sexing and I sit or walk
alone seeking other Gods who have forsaken you —
and we will sit together and walk together and
mate together... And you will sit and walk and
mate together. You kept us from one another and we
too — yes we kept you — each we kept from that
destiny, that destiny high or low... now goodbye, au
revoir — soft mediocrity yours. And ours — lunacy
or................. Godhood.

Sometimes I sit waiting, sometimes I go out
looking, sometimes I'm busy preparing, always for
love, though.

And it isn't fair — it isn't fair — why did they
do it? I didn't ask to happen — there was no pain —
nothing — then they made me and taught me to be
afraid — taught me to hate love, beauty, life, myself
— taught me to hate myself — the sweet loveliness of
being — a human being — epitome — taught me sex is
dirty — girls are dangerous — taught me to want shit —
crappy jobs, cars, houses, clothes — yes, clothes make

10

the man — clothes make the man. You insipid jerk
who made the clothes — you trivial ass who made the
cars — the houses — the cities. But they're all
bigger than we are, aren't they? We're nothing
and this junk — is something? You taught me this
and I'll never forget it — never forget it — it'll
haunt me till the blood lies still in my veins — and
I go quiet — terror — it's racking my guts — eating me
up — I run yes I run from window to window —
looking for something true out there — holding my
stomach — like a guy who stopped a slug — and the
pain is eating me — eating me up — you dirty bastards,
you did this to me — why, all I want is to live but
I can't — I can't without you — I need the love you
can't give — you need my love — it frightens you —
can it frighten? Yes, I saw it happen — yes, they
told us love was for sissies — or God — or a mother
or a daddy — or a wife — but for people — no, not
for people. No position, no category, people. Their
love can't fit a mold — you can't call it mother love
or love for country — only love, love, love clean and
unlabeled — no, not to be used by politicians — and
statesmen for war and tax — not to be used by busyness men for Christmas and Valentine's Day — poor
Christ! Poor St. Valentine! — but to be given — yes,
given — to another lover. Who is a lover? Where do
you find a lover? — Lover, lover, giver, lover, give
love, love give — please — take my love. No? You don't
want it — you don't want it — why? — Please take it —
there's no security in it — no safe strings leading
to and from — too too much freedom — doesn't fit the
mold — can't be categorized — cashed in — can't be
cashed — no payoff with my love — no payoff — not
negotiable — not tangible — sorry — God! Am I sorry...
Love is like an electrical current and people
should be wired together and if people were wired
together there would be complete circuits and juice
flowing from one to another and then back again
from one to another and then back again and the

loss is negligible the loss is negligible. It's not like that — it's not — it just isn't — when you open your switch and let the current flow out into the world out out out then you see their switches are all closed all closed closed and the sweet juice has no place to go — it tries — it really tries — frantically, but no takers — all the switches are closed. Now I'm empty, empty of love — all gone-spent-dispersed-dispensed-ejaculated — and hate fills me and my face fills with hate and you read it and run and I call you by your true name — imbecile, idiot, coward, fool, lost one, oh beautiful, beautiful flesh — beauty flesh with closed switches — beautiful I kneel — yes genuflect to you... Beauty-full flesh give me an alternative... please. It isn't fair. It isn't fair.

Come... listen to the dreamer, the idealist, the impractical unrealistic one; with ideas unworkable in this modern world. Ideas and ideals certain to lead you to chaos and dissension, turmoil and conflict — or heaven. Yes, heaven, if

such a thing has been, is, or could be, then it is here and now; not on some gold-plated, thick-carpeted, air-conditioned cloud city with excellent plumbing — a place mortally unattainable, unknowable. Listen — we of the flesh, here is our heaven and here our hell. Come... share my vision — follow this thought-path leading —

leading where? Out this madness? Yes, I know your fear. Leaving the security of the known. Perhaps I've seen more of the madness — but try.

Perhaps I see more — but try. Can't you see your pain is now your comfort? Your pain is like an old friend who long ago stopped giving you pleasure, and the tedium and the boredom set in so gradually

and increased so gradually that if exposed to it suddenly, it would be unbearable.

"Sure I know he's an idiot, but I've known him for so long! Why, we were friends in school — I can't be cruel."

Cruel hell! Don't talk to me of cruelty, your pleasurable self-destruction is sickening to me. If your mind would become clear, crystal-clear as an always fresh, always renewing, sparkling mountain

stream... you can't let idiots with muddy minds go
wading through it. Old friends!?!

I refuse to die here. To die in modern society
is one of the most degrading experiences imaginable.
It's illegal to just die — just die and go back to
the soil. It's illegal — really. There are a group
among us: the modern ghouls... the undertakers —
they haunt buildings called mortuaries. These
ineffectual sadists, mother-father cutters, rapists,
incestuous dead-body diddlers, blood-pumpers, cotton-
cheek-stuffing, ghoul make-up artists — o to hell
with 'em, I don't even want to discuss them — let's
just give our bodies back to the soil.

A thick skull is a sick skull.

Funny, I just read one of those articles: the
kind that magazines feature so often. This one
about what they called the problem of Heart Trouble
and Sex. I don't know if your imagination is as
vivid as mine but this one threw me into laughing
tantrums. They soundproofed a room, got a couple
of couples — young married ones — fastened pulse
recording and other electronic equipment to "their"
equipment; turned out the lights and said go... and
go they did — all for science. Everybody got their
gun and the magazine got their article. C'mon all
kinds of guys with bad pumps have died while
fuckin' — only question is — was it or wasn't it worth
it? These commercial writers are really too much
aren't they?

Well anyway — they recorded pulse rates as
high as 170 on those fuckers for science — when the
average is 72, and pointed out the hell that plays
with a bad heart and how many guys die that way
and how tough it gets psychologically — when you
want to go, but are afraid. No way! No busy "business"
life for me, no hustle-bustle life with its ulcerated

14

lace curtain stomach and sloppy heart valves. Like
I said, let's lie on the beach this afternoon, get
some sun, we'll run up to the rocks at Malibu, after
I'll buy you a yogurt... happy balling kiddies.

I've been trying to talk St. Peter into
canonizing Satan, BUT HE RESOLUTELY REFUSES. Seems
in the millennium-fold statutes — somewhere in the
deep dank archives of ecclesiastical law — canonization
can only be performed upon the deceased, and when
we talk of eliminating Lucifer, he gets fidgety and
shifty-eyed and very suspicious, I think he knows
that I know. I suppose I should be more cautious:
another inquisition would finish me. Ah, forget it,
I'd rather die than shut up and shut down the Mind.

Today the screaming in the streets hurt my
ears again; I tore up my brain and the head pain
again; came back to my room again; locked the door
again; pulled the covers over my head again;
masturbated again.

God, I wish you were true.

They-are-coming-closer-and-closer-with-their-
razor-edge-apathy-for-my-red-pulsing-throat-Why-do-
they-want-to-kill-me-when-I-snatch-death-from-their-
minds-I-hear-their-blood-smelling-footsteps-pounding-
sounding-hollow-dead-end-I-am-very-tired-don't-cry-
they-will-be-quick.

People would say, "You two are so much alike,
how do you stand each other?"

Opposites attract... who's kidding who? If you
believe in yourself, the basic substance of yourself,
what can you do with your opposite? If really
opposite, they can't be much more than a curio — and

what has this to do with "love yourSelf?" So many
seem to feel that the spontaneous affinity you
feel, when you observe and contact in another
person a belief or an attitude that you see as
precious in yourself, that this is a negative thing,
an unhealthy reaction. Look! If I dig Ellington
or Debussy, it's because they talk to me; I should
be attracted to those who don't or can't? No — I
believe in mySelf. I believe in my evaluation of
what I see and hear. If someone shows an interest
in me, give her or him credit for being discerning
at least. The outspoken ones, those who lay it on
the line, not afraid to say, "This is me — take it or
leave it — if you don't like it, okay tell me about
it. If you've got something to say and enough guts
to declare yourself, I'll listen for awhile — I know
you could be right — I know that I have been wrong,
will be wrong — don't like it, being wrong. Tell
me, I may fight you, probably will, but I'm worth
straightening out."

And that's the thing... you feel that they
are worth it, worth the effort. Obviously, few are.
But if they are, they're that rare thing — a human
being in growth, in flux, and well worth a kick in
the ass. Don't worry, these people you don't hurt...
all sinewy inside, strong enough with the knowledge
of Self-worth. If they don't put a high evaluation
on you, your efforts to hip them will only be
laughable... If that even.

This thing of being wrong reminds me of Hank:
he and Huru, his Japanese girlfriend, rent my little
downstairs studio up here on Lookout Mountain Road
in Laurel Canyon: a sweet guy who would like to
paint but can't let himself go, even after years of
technical training, even after years of analysis-
style therapy. He makes his living doing renderings
for architects: those insipid watercolors of proposed
buildings architects show to prospective clients.

He's an intelligent guy who loves himself and
hates himself for it — Yeah!

How many are fighting this one out? Well, it
stopped him dead. LOVES HIMSELF AND HATES HIMSELF
FOR IT, and what else could he do with Old-World
Italian background and Catholic beginning; a
brother who wants to become a priest — What chance?
O well, like Mr. Mortimer Sahl says... Onward.

A day I'm digging around in the yard for a
stash I'd buried (I never did find it) and casual
dialoguing with Hank — probably about abstract
painting, a mutual interest — when I'd remarked
that I'd been wrong about something — some incident,
I don't remember what, and what a drag it was.

He jumped me, "What's so bad about being wrong?"

That stops me dead. These things always come
at me like out of another world... and they really
are. I have to shake my head, re-orient myself —
this is the way they think!

I say, "Well, when you goof you blow the
moment."

"Huh?"

"Look, Hank, can you see that life is a thing
of moments, or say incidents happening one right
after the other, sometimes it seems with practically
no continuity, like maybe a badly cut film, with
scenes randomly sequenced, seemingly unrelated one
to the other. But nonetheless each has emotional
content, the potential to express extremes of joy or
hate they should express or, more generally,
extremes of passivity."

Hank's quiet awhile, then he kinda clears his
throat and says, "Now this form of empiricizing is
of course impossible other than on a very superficial
idealistic plane; a really well-intellectualized
idealism comprehends through and beyond this quite
easily..."

I cut in, "Whoa, what the fuck is all this

incoherent crap? Sounds like something plagiarized from a third-rate Huxley imitation... look, Hank, like this... driving, wanna make a left turn, car coming opposite side, you turn, mind's elsewhere, depth perception all off, miscalculate speed... suddenly heart pushing your tonsils; screech... Carrrruuummmblang tinkle tinkle blood all over the place... man you were wrong! Like it's not nice, you goofed the moment.

"Want more? Okay, say right now standing here, some crazy looking chick comes walking up the Canyon and she's under full sail, fully-rigged, heels, Chanel-cut suit, a straight kinda boutique hat... ok you know how to handle this type: like a wild man — into the pad, off the sandals, off the sweatshirt, the jeans, on the twenty dollar sport shirt, new-cut slacks, gold mesh belt, Filipino shoes — all that Xmas stuff you thought you'd never wear and you catch her two doors up... man, the chick's a non-objective painter of note — new from NY, the Village, visiting a sister up the street, who ranked her day, draped her in same-size square clothes, drug and dragged her to a Valley wedding reception but she just couldn't cut it, split — one thing in mind: get home and out of uniform. And now this yo-yo comes sliding up to hit on her, you're dressed like you're out looking for a wedding reception. Too tired to even put you down — just totterlytilts onto her sandals. And man you were wrong! You'd stopped a beat and Seen, you'd've Seen that something about her is out of sync and probably even figured the situation and conducted Self properly. But no! You goofed and it's the biggest drag in life! Sure a growing person gleans lots of what they know from mistakes but that shit's gotta start stopping somewhere. Let's face it when people pick themselves up and dusting off say, 'Well, it was good experience, I had to learn' — stick

around: usually you'll see it's a repetitious thing.
Like I say if you're alive and learning, you learn
and life starts getting fun — after awhile things
begin to click. What's wrong with being wrong? Wow!"

O at times how I hate my trivial paltry petty
drip-shit world.

Even Einstein became a monster... how Jewish
he must have felt when he composed that letter to
Roosevelt, "We can raise hell," he said, and did...
and the stench of the ovens ceased. Yes, in the
biggest stench of man-flesh of all ages... the ovens
ceased. And Jews stopped nerve-jumping in the fires
of Auschwitz and Japanese began molecules melting
in the fires of Hiroshima and Nagasaki. And now
sweet kind Albert — gentle soul we honor you. Thank
you for hell kind-eyed old man who became less
human and more Jew... as all those who became less
human and more gentile and more Aryan and more
black and more brown and more blue and more pink
and more red... and more ashes.

If you think a young girl more beautiful
than the old man half-eaten by cancer; a bouquet
of roses more beautiful than a pile of feces; a new
fat tire more beautiful than an old lacy worn flat
one; if you think the crystal-clean Miami Beach
walk more beautiful than the vomit and mucus-
spittle smeared skid-row walk... then I say you are
frightened, have never really looked into beauty —
don't know what you call beautiful or ugly are only
effect and the cause — pure beauty. Yes, the cold
relentless irrefutable laws of this-makes-that, the
gorgeously impersonal laws of pus and scabs, fire
and water, drop and break and the flaming cometed
geometrical warp of the cosmos.
If you think he more beautiful than she, or

she than he, or his than hers, or hers than his — if
you would be alive... your hope lies as much in the
dissonant decayed, as in the melodic ripe lush flesh;
each only the end and result of truth; wonderfully
functional, believable, dependable, omnipresent
truth.

Truth... the good friend, the sire of your
rotten ovary... your breath-stenching, fuming,
congested, gaseous colon.

Truth... the good friend, the sire of the
lovely, coordinated, rhythmic, happy pulse and flow
and glow of your healthiness.

Do you cry often little man? I cry often — yes.
Why do you cry little man? I cry for my world and
the human blood smeared across its face. I cry for
the hate in my brothers for themselves. I cry each
time anew, yes each time anew I see him standing
whimpering, for a soft spot searching himself, and
the sharp hate thing in the other hand — ready.

Astronomical I.Q. Kathy: Mensa member, good
typist, good speller, good critic, good fat-girl
Friday. Knows about commas and colons, proper
sentence structure and such — types my manuscripts
for me. A someday-would-like-to-write-girl — and a
long twisty road it'll be, and sweet and sick and
digs my work and me.

We're sitting in one of those immaculate
chrome-and-glass cafés, where you can watch them
under sterile conditions, by a sterile chef, prepare
your sterile food in sterile cookery. These garish
short-order houses with their short-lived clientele,
are scattered all over Hollywood. They have a
similarity of smell and architecture and name I
find amusing: Huffs, Puffs, Nuffs, Snookys, Gookys,
Pukies... o well! She's told me of her plan to see a
physician, "I don't feel well, run down all the time,

no energy, no vitality, always listless — I need a
shot or something." While she was talking, telling
me about her doctor and her condition, I watched her
eat, looked at her food. She ate listlessly. Who could
blame her? That greasy mess she was surrounding
could give her nothing. Could it give her life? It
was dead, devitalized, filled the void for the
moment; soon hunger would come again, more fat,
more hunger, more fat... no life, no vitality, no
strength.

Call the doctor. "Doctor I'm ill, it hurts
here, my bowels don't move, got no energy, my head
aches." Look girl, like this: TB, polio, cancer, what's
the difference? All the diseases are shit. What did
you expect, laying around, eating shit? "Doctor,
this cold, it's killing me, hangs on, can't seem to
clear it up. Doctor, I'm tired, always tired..."

Sure you come off so stupid; why be such an
idiot. Get hip. Snap! Go organic girl, get into
salads and simple stuff. And hey, fill the lungs,
let the good air and sun cleanse away the dark-
dank-dwelling bad-bugs.

Activate or deteriorate. Eat vital be vital.
(Slogans yet!) I nod at a guy sitting across the
room. "Look at him there, with his gut hanging past
his genitals, chins down to his navel, legs and ass
swollen till body hung loose as strings on an old
out-of-tune instrument — like all things not used
they just deteriorate and die..."

"I know you're talking really about me."

"Well, what if I am — course I am. It's only to
say don't go that way."

"What do you want me to do?"

"Do? Run, yes run, jump, yes jump. Roll and
tumble like all live things, like puppies and
children — yes, before they're told, 'Be dignified,
act like a little lady. Nice boys aren't so rough,
now don't get dirty, act like a little man, be good

children.' Yes, nice — yes kiddies kill your exuberance, kill your young joy, build your inhibition and start rotting like Mommy and Daddy. Hell I was 30 before I knew a girl ever farted."

"What would the neighbors say if I went running 'round the block? The boss would think I'm off if I dressed like you, he'd have a talk with me."

"To hell with them — tell 'em to shove it... stop buying into all this quadrilateral repression. When a culture, when the stodgy style of a society, maintaining it, becomes more important than the physical and mental health of the individuals who comprise it; if it's detrimental to their physical and emotional health, when its stupidities become more important than the individual's health... then pass, forget it, or you're a gone one. And the doctors — forget it — neither you nor they can pump life with a hypo... for a little, yes, a short flight, but you always come down farther than you went up."

Suddenly, as I sat there, stoned one night, I knew why her rooms sometimes would frighten me so — she lived with Death. There He is... Beast sitting on the arm of her chair, hand gently resting upon her shoulder... I feel a thousand little bumps rise on my flesh and the hairs at the back of my neck troubled. And then the radio too — strangely somber and heavy with His music. I smell the beginnings of decay... these lines I jot and hand them to her. Carefully she reads and carefully she lays down the scrap of paper. Not a crack in the mask and begins talking of a Degas exhibit we'd seen.

I didn't go back for awhile. Finished a story and needed a typist who could turn out a readable draft and was sure she was no-hope dead. And writer and corpse began work on another book.

There's a passivity thick in the air — I feel
its musty tentacles reaching — smell its rot — o
unholy unholy — o for sharper stronger tools:
plodding determined worker-in-art that I am — and
the Saturday night doppler effect of laughter from
open convertibles speeding up Lookout Mountain Road
going partying and all the time all this life
whizzing by my typewriter and half my mind
yearning sniffing at its wake — and all the
mechanical maze of clickety clickety old beat-up
Smith-Corona and piling stacks of manuscripts and
editing and blurry eye fatigue between them and me
and you and me — time time time o stop I don't want
to die sitting here alone two-finger-type-shouting
into the dark.

I see you, the pretty facade hinders me
little — so run — run back glad to the unknowing
ones. You want your buttons pushed — sorry, can't
make the scene. You don't want an artist. You need a
father type or an executive type or a political type
or a...? Shit, you need someone who must lead, must
direct, run things — run you. A robot button-pusher
for robot button-pushees — and you love it, so you
should be very happy together, you two... and o the
night is sweet, someone's phonograph is playing
'Rite of Spring' it fills the air and me and I stop —
always for beauty. No musical robot Stravinsky or
Bartok or Hindemith — those guys, if they had
buttons that had to be pushed, they pushed them...
true of all greatly creative people. And I always
felt hungry and always went to the refrigerator —
but there wasn't any love there either... and the
telephone, incessantly trespassing: tearing in half
our conversations, our recorded concertos, our
moments of reverie, of passion — and the constant
phone intrigue: "o why did I answer that damned
phone? That was the one person I didn't want to

talk to, will you tell whoever calls next I'm not
in. If Frank calls, I've gone down to the Laurelite,
I can't talk to him till I hear what Jacques thinks.
Whoever else calls I'm in Palm Springs until
Thursday — Oh is that Stephen? No let me speak to
him; I'm sure he can help me with Mrs. Rianaldo,
who said she'd try and introduce me to Count
Alphonse who's the boyfriend of Patricia D'Leny who
wants to read my manuscript, her husband is Ralph
D'Leny; you know, he's that publishing office
downstairs."

And then this Billy Graham-type character
comes boomshouting out of the radio — fantastically
aggressively preaching passivity — and my mother
pity-laughing-sad says, "Poor people..." And then
there's the guy who says, "Yes, I always wanted to
write, could have too, but then Emily and I, just
out of college and we were married and the kids
right away, you know — and expenses! You don't
realize how those expenses pile up when you raise a
family." Yes I do buster: membership in country clubs
and two cars and big-screen TV's are expensive... and
the insipid complaining incompetent is just as
intensely pursuing his true want as the most
dynamic power executive pursues his... and we
passed a car on the freeway; there were three women
riding — temperature 90 degrees in the shade. They
were dressed in gowns of black with hoods of black
covering their heads, leaving only the face and
hands out in the air... I shuddered, looked at
Diane, she said, "They're Nuns." I agreed with her.
The nomenclature was exact — a Nun is a none is a
none. Oh I guess Catholicism is a good thing as
Americanism is a good thing and all ism's and
philosophies and credos and codes are good things
and the shit is piled high tonight my dear ones...
and strange the way they laugh at me! I don't
laugh at them; the way they tie themselves in all

secure, everything in place: tight shoes, hats, collars, vests, corsets, garters... pancake make-up, everything covered, concealed, under control. And those jockey shorts, the way they pull the balls and cock in so nice and tight — under control — that's it kiddies, nothing flopping loose like that wonderful girl and the way her breasts free-moved in rhythm with her body as she walked... how good! No, honey, it's vulgar — here's your Maidenform bra — snub 'em in, tie 'em down... no idiot, don't burn the book. Remember our agreement — throw it in the street — might still get to somebody. And Johnny and I, top down tire squealing up Laurel Canyon and this guy in another MG giving us the sports car drivers' salute: the casual wave, the IN-club acknowledgement of another of their kind... I stand up and finger-yell "Fuck you." What else can you say to some inane, presumptuous clown who categorizes you, accepts you because you drive the same type of car — they're not kidding either. But then it's all hopeless anyway — Jags never wave at MG's. But then shit, Ferraris never wave at Jags.

The secret ones... there's a look, when you see it, be afraid. Secret look of concealment — you can feel them, sitting inside there, back behind the eyes, looking out. The face calm, composed, cool, unemotional but behind the eyes — behind the "nice," twisted with hate, mouth snarl-curled, lips gore-drooling. This face wants to, will — will kill. Back away slowly, no quick moves, don't look alarmed, suspicious, frightened, keep backing — now run — for life. Don't look back, never ever. Don't go back — to be consumed, eaten alive. It's a beast, crazed, frothing rabid ego, maddened by inhibition, repression. Sad, yes all of them sad. Leave them to heaven; leave them to Uncle Sigmund... o what beautiful, talented liars.

Yes, they live alone with their secrets. Can't let you know what's going on in there or you could plan your strategy perfectly. To them life is like a card game or an infantry battle, a thing of bluffs, feints, subterfuge, false facades; a whole closetful of disassorted masks and costumes. Impossible for them to really believe that there are people who mean them no harm, have no want or need to destroy or control, people who couldn't be bothered to get one up on you, to beat you down even if you told them how.

Do you step on the sidewalk cracks? Or never? Do you step on ants? Or can't you ever? The all and everything of you is there, I mistype kike for like and understanding comes out understabing. Yes... the book of self is plainly written but hard to read so close to the eye.

And reasoning is perhaps — like an appendix or ten toes — an experiment of nature's to be accepted or rejected by evolution. And just as superfluous and confusing and frightening and isolating to the mass when encountered in itself by a member of same. Frontal-lobe surgery being the most practical saving solution.

Den splen flen gen zen... Zen actors, Zen babies, Zen writers, Zen whores. Another door to open, another hook to get hung on. Zen, like all these philosophical streams, can only lead you to the sea: the vast, boundless, shoreless sea of Understanding, Lucidity, Enlightenment. Many rivers to the Cosmic Sea: large and small, mud-choked and fast sparkle rivers.

So few who let the mind follow the thought-stream to Enlightenment, to their own minute or great Sea of Understanding. So few to follow the mind's logical sequential progress through Life's uncharted twists and turns of danger strewn

freeform. Easier to stay in the safely banked river
world, the Zen stream or the Christianity stream or
the... what's the difference? — If it's tagged it's
the constricting... stream. And how comforting to be
labeled and how tiring to keep your same-place in
the river, upcurrent swimming all through long
tedious days and nights of a static-still life — with
its stagnant spirit — with its prematurely withered
face and soul. And upstream swimming to keep your
safe philosophic place is your own self's hell-
sentence.

In freeform, even the Sea cannot hold you...
sucked up you are and raised and rained into another
"called differently" stream and over and over and
each time the river clearer, the sea vaster and over
and over and perhaps after Death.

Are you a writer? No, I'm a man who sometimes
writes. Yes, a man first — painter, bricklayer, bank
clerk, Christian or Hindu — man first or nothing. "I
vote the straight democratic ticket, just like my
old man and his father before him — and my kid, he'll
vote it too. Yesireee we'll see to that, we're real
democrats — eh, maw!"

"And then I found God! What a wonderful
peace I have now, such tranquility. You know I
haven't been angry once, not once since that day
when I knew Mister Graham was talking just to me.
I'm Saved. I'm reborn. And you know I don't care
whether Frank calls ever again or not — besides I'm
ashamed of the things we did, but I've confessed
all that... to HIM."

"Oh Mabel! Listen kid, you know that cute
actor you were asking me about; you know the one
who did such a good job in that Kramer picture —
y'know what? He said he couldn't act at all till he
got into Bahai, didn't know it but he couldn't.
They're having a meeting at his place tonight — what
say we go?"

Have you tried the Tao of Zen or... O heavens to Betsy! What to say about all this! But then I suppose you can see it all anyway.

Zensy zpensy flensey frensey and you think I'm putting it down — well I'm not. All that crud is great, long as you don't get hooked. A religion or philosophy is horse-shit unless it's open-ended and could even lead you out of itself. Course I don't know any that intend this, but I know people who have done them and kicked 'em and came out better people. I'm one.

Send the cover from this book (along with ten cents to cover cost of mailing) and I'll send you our new Rosicrucifier's Illustrated Brochure on how with this mental imaging thing you c'n get the boss' job and a new Caddy and castles and all kinds of stuff. We can hip you to the real secret of the universe and all that. Like we just accidentally stumbled onto this secret of the ancient swingers. If you own your own home... no money down and payments don't start till next year for this easy to understand, do-it-yourself course. And remember, all the great Rosicrucifiers have had lots of magnetism for chicks — so do it now today. Write for the GOLDEN door to opportunity.

Well yes... but it all seems so unrelated to modern life, complicated modern life, Phi Beta Kappa and time payments... yes, I know. Teddy, rough and ready Teddy, says, "If it's good to me, it's good for me," which means to him: if I like it, it's good for me. And he leads a pretty rough life, gets high a lot, drinks fairly heavily, generally lives it up; a lovable — though 'times chicken-shit guy, who gets as much or more out of life than most. But he's young, I said, "Crazy — live, but do one thing for me will you? When at thirty-five or when I don't know but nevertheless when your insides are dropping out

your anus, you're wearing glasses, false teeth, you
can't get a hard-on and you're flipping out — Kill
yourself will you? Don't come around bugging me
about your problems. Sure I know I look ridiculous
to you with my sunbathing, my weightlifting, my
raw foods, driving ten miles to get spring water —
in my sweatsuit, night running through the hills —
with my disdain of lush and smoke and all the rest
of it, but man I'm virile, I have more endurance
than lots of guys half my age, don't have headaches
anymore, not bothered by the messy confusion of
little illness that I was so prone to with what I
suppose you'd call my delicate constitution. But
baby, most important of all I want to keep having
sex as long as I'm around. The idea of senility —
never again consummating the tender-wild thing
with a girl, hurts me even to think about it.
Imagine — never again to feel her delicious warmth
way up inside or the matchless grace of lovely
expressive fingers caressing my erection. Sorry
kids... Hand me the wheat germ."

Yes I suppose I knew what would happen.
What I would do when I first saw the man and the
child. She, the child, not beautiful but attractive,
attractive in the important sense, nothing to do
with features really, with eyes, nose, mouth; these
were all there, and I was going to say there was a
symmetry about them. I know now, of course, though
I haven't seen her since, that she was ugly. Ugly.
And this is difficult for me at times, difficult to
see from Society's perspective, from their point of
view. You see, I'm an outcast. So you must realize
that it might not be an easy thing for me to tell
that which is ugly from that which is beautiful,
except for myself; and I'm an outcast. Yes, she
would be ugly. But the way she stopped to stroke
the little puppy cowering there in the doorway, you

could see — well, I could see love. And the puppy, he could feel the love. She was quite lovely, kneeling for that brief moment, with her tone and hand telling the little animal of human love and kindness, perhaps for the first time — perhaps for the last. The man spoke her name. I can't remember it now, but I recall quite clearly the sound and feeling, the sound and feeling of his voice, the — I don't know really. I suppose I must have heard and felt this voice before. How else can I explain that I understood the man from such a small thing? Boredom was the thing he felt. There was much of this, along with other things too — perhaps impatience. But this means nothing in itself, though they were there when he called the child from the puppy. My delight in the small dog and child and understanding was not felt by the man. Indeed, I saw, looking intently upon his face, this would never be felt. Can you perhaps understand the sorrow I felt for him, the man, when just then I could feel the emptiness of his life?

Can you understand the elation of hearing her voice? Oh, it was full with sweetness and joys and had little bells tingling around its edges — her answer had all of these and, yes, more, and yes too, a strain of melancholy, a poignance, a melancholy running through there, through the sound of bells. Perhaps it will be difficult for you to believe — though it is true, quite true; once in a while, not often but once in a while I seem to see very clearly. A man's eyes may brush across mine and he's gone, he's gone but I know him, his saintliness, his evil, all, all of him I know. For an infinitesimal point in time I am he and I know, I could tell you of many such instances, yes, with animals too, yes, more frequently with animals. Like the time at the sea when watching the gull. How gracefully he wheeled and rode the wind, how

effortlessly. So intently I watched him, I remember.
And then it happened. I was him. It was very good,
so free, completely free; and the other thing — there
was no hate, no hate at all. Quite unusual, really,
but then to be that free — of course — I would like
to tell you more, but this is only so you might
understand about the man and the little girl —
how I know. Those dissonances of melancholy I
understood — you see that I would. And I wanted to
cry. But people stop to look when I cry. And I did
so want to follow the little girl; I couldn't, you
know, if they were all looking at me the way they
do; so I didn't. Oh I wish you could have been there
too. I wish all of the good people could have been
there. I love to follow butterflies, they do such
happy, full-of-life things. Though this was much
more fun; she was, you see, the first angel I'd ever
seen. When they went into the fruit market, it was
wonderful. It was the same wherever they went, but
there in the fruit market such a funny thing
happened, such a nice thing too. The man in the
white apron who takes your money was quite angry
with one of the people. They were shouting at each
other and were really quite nasty with each other
concerning money or something like that. When we
came up to the counter (the man and the girl I
mean) my attention was on the two men. They were
so loud, and I could feel the violence gathering —
I usually can. When it gets like this, people
sometimes hit each other. If that happens, I
usually go away, because it frightens me. Oh, I
wish you could have seen it, what happened then.
The child laid the fruit they had chosen on the
counter, and I remember how solemnly she looked at
the angry man as she touched him on the arm to
bring his attention to the fruit they had chosen. I
knew she felt no fear at all. I got the feeling she
just wasn't attuned to the violence. The man spun on

her to do or say — what I don't know. But whatever, with him so full of hate, it would be ugly of course. Well, he stopped, stopped breathing, stopped moving, and for a moment he just went into her eyes; he went very deep very fast. What the hate, poison dissipated to I don't know; but tranquility moved through him and across his face. His movements as he made their change were all serenity. I remember that, as I followed the man and the little girl out to the street, the two men spoke something and laughed together; it was that soft love-laugh I seldom hear between men. I followed them a few blocks to a house, and when they went inside I sat on the curb at the other side of the street to watch the house and to think about the man and girl. It wasn't that he was evil; it was, I knew, because of his fear that he couldn't understand or feel the child. To the man, an ugly child was disappointing. I know men — they love beautiful children. It is sad, but it is difficult for them to accept an arrangement of physical characteristics that they consider not pleasing. Yes, it was sad. I remember as I sat there — I sat a long time, it got dark — I didn't mind 'cause I kept thinking and feeling the sadness of this thing: the man and the child. And of the child. She knew. She knew of the man's disappointment, she knew of his shame of her before other men. Now there is something I should tell you. You might not know this. Angels can be hurt, and they can be bent too; they can be twisted too. I know, I've seen the thing happen; and it was when I remembered the delicacy, the tender vulnerability of angels that I began to weep for the child. And like always, people stopped to stare, and a few laughed when they found me crying there under the street light, I know they didn't know about the angel, but still it made me feel strange. In the house a light came on and I

could see a woman placing food upon a table, and
then the man and child came in. They sat and began
to eat. I liked watching the little girl. It was very
nice. So I just sat and kept looking like that...

SALLEE

At nineteen I'd never really thought about actually meeting one; they were from that other world of blue-tinted swimming pools, long expensive convertibles — a world I'd seen in films and magazines. But I came home that summer night in 1939, my buddies had commandeered the place and had thrown an impromptu party to celebrate my getting a job — which I'd already quit. And there she was sitting on the edge of my parents' dining-room table. The perfectly formed face and body and crossed nylons showing good — that "See I'm beautiful, the world is mine" carriage I knew from fan magazines. I was nineteen — an unworldly naive nineteen. She was fourteen — an incredulous precocious fourteen — already working, high fashion model. She fell in love with my eyes and manner, I with her everything — which she had exactly... yes.

Sallee Music her name was and she had eyes only for me and I for her, it was like this for our next thirteen years — thirteen years of dramatic separating and together coming. We were wired for sex, charged with the stuff. Romantic love. Yes, like a true confessions story or the movies of Jennifer Jones or the poetry of Walter Benton — only we lived it — were it. We were romance — we breathed the stuff — it was all ecstasy. Even the paining goodbye-forevers were only a breather, a physical and emotional replenishing. All pleasure, rich sensual pleasure. We never got to know each other, there was no need, no time, too drugged with erotica. I remember though, after Movie Mogul Howard Hughes signed her and Hollywood columnist Louella O named her The High School Cinderella

Girl of Los Angeles, she scared me some. Wasn't till years later that I actually got over that awe of the "Glamour" world and its denizens. But she didn't know... I was very cool. Still she loved me. Still I couldn't believe in myself, couldn't really go after what I wanted. Yet she did, knew there was someone important in there if I would only bring it out. All through our time it was like that — she was the aggressor. She was into life. Never passive. Soon as she was 16 she bought herself a new '41 Chevy sport coupe and she'd come by honking me out and laughing her beautiful laugh to see me. But after we're married (which, a few years into our relationship, was the *only* way she'd go on with it) then it was "get a job." I'd tried jobs. Hated them. Music (singing, playing) was all I wanted. But still too passive and unbelieving in self to just go after it. Truth is I hadn't found my Way in the world and anyway wasn't ever really right for the girl. She married an actor-type director the day our divorce was final — became a Catholic — "I know, I know!" But, in the ruthlessness of untempered youth, I stamped a lot of the guts out of her and she always kind of wanted to get in line anyway and I, the eternal misfit, never did... Hating self when I did. And so hating her some for wanting me to and she me some for not doing it, all so everydaylike, and sad.

I remember her, too, one time toward the end she came to see me, I knew she was in doubt, hadn't seen her in weeks — she'd escaped into her modeling, movie new-friends, gobbled up by glamour. But I kept tapping at the back of her brain and also still much hooked by the ovaries she said, "Come for a drive with me."

By then after weeks of no Sallee, I was so empty of her I'd have gone anywhere just to breathe her in. She drove quietly, neither of us spoke, good to be close again. She stopped the car at our quiet, many-memoried, back road place and said, "Kiss me."

"Wow! You can get rough can't you Sallee. Got to test yourself, pleeeeease baby, easy." I was mumbling something else about being fair and all when her face filled my world — we stayed that way for minutes, hours, days... Who cared? She was toying to a degree but that stopped right off, everything stopped, really everything the whole hassling hassled world — no planning calculating cooling nothing but our pulling each other tighter and tighter — hurting — the hurting more intensifying the thing, it was as though we'd never release each other, never let go, as though we'd found something of such tremendous magnitude all striving was trite.

I hadn't yet learned to keep a running objective view of things. What's going on? I was a romantic. Totally. She was much more of a pragmatist, figuring things. Yeah she'd go after what she wanted. She'd go after the truth of things and deal with it. We had found it — poor children — we had. We had known it all — played the music — together sounded the coupling communicable crescendo. But couldn't know. It was much much too much for us. Too young. We couldn't grasp the significance — to feel this at-one-with-love life is so against our indelible feelings of long-learned insignificance.

Strange as I write this, ponder in retrospect, the moment is with me, strong with me again. I remember we sat for a long time not moving, said nothing; there was nothing else to say. We had never either of us spoken so profoundly before, or ever together did again.

How seldom known... The sweet kuming, the no-game kuming, sweet juicing together. So tired I was and am of contrived trying tiddly-wink mental sex, so long between animal hard-ons... Well perhaps if I

just kissed those flower honey lips... oh yes we
had no reasoning then — how simple everything and
how far away the humdrum tedium of argue and
complaint. Oh how big it would be to have it all —
all the reasoning and the animal thing too, the
lust hot and pull the mind and physical images,
like in a viewfinder, together. Why else be human,
we animal-gods, to work on the dull edge of life
with the keen edge of mind, to bring the total of
sharpness into experience, to feel it all more; the
full dominion of intensity, the sheer loveliness in
complete abandoned involvement in life, in lovesex,
of being lost in these things and so finding them...
Ah, yes, hummm. That once in a while thing — the
tender afterness of a she and I lost identity
moment — those few so seldom moments.

A kuming together... She and I in Love...
Yes... deep and our loving was many-timed the
fullness I speak of. I remember the electric
feeling — electric, like a positive and negative
current it was. Yes, her opulent flesh come-eyed me,
sucked my breath to see it move about edible and
with eyes touching and hands touching and kissing
and rubbing... A mind-body caress... A beautiful
thing, softly gentle-wild and frantic thing —
clinging forms warm and wet together and sweet
juice in mouths and hair, oh yes closer love closer,
touch there and yes, here... Let us silky-glide me
into you, through you, over surround around
consume you and oh yes dear one like that, yes
trembly way snug in there close and around, all
hardness and softness and more and more and deep
deep deep somewhere in singleness of flesh and
soul... A fragile delicate swelling joy touches a
sensual tone and the tone soft-shivers waves of
sound of color of nerve-tremblings that ripple
through and through... Then all-encompassing
current, lashes and gales through our quivering

38

onebody, with lips touching and the sweet current
spurting from our sexes into one another, and
tearing through us and crackling arcing and
sparking between our lips... And again racing
tingling through us... Ah good good good — and
slower slo slo and again and again quicker... from
cock to cunt to lips again and again... It's the
body electric sex-circuitry of sweet orgasmic Love...
the completedness — the close closed circuitry of
ultimate Love kuming... O what sweet Truth is in
Love... And such a delicate pastel hallowed after-
lost she-and-I moment.

And I knew Wilhelm Reich was right — but for
me only in love.

The mind : The soul : The spirit : The
personality : The flesh : The filling : The void :
The emotion : The intellect : The Individuality of
every son of Adam, of every daughter of Eve...

like a broken coin — worthless without its fitting
other part.

Sallee was always after me to stop picking my
nose, said it showed no class, that it was just a
nervous symptom; I always came up with something
though. She had it — "class" — the kind she meant
when she used the word — loaded with it.
I remember once, someone gave her an old coat,

some kind of animal skin — hell, she cut that thing short, made a wide belt with the scraps; it was wild and when she put it on she'd touch it here and there moving things and it became her. I remember we used to lie in bed — I'd talk for hours — she loved to listen. Sometimes my voice gets very good, kinda soft mellow quality when I don't have to project it, talking to someone close like that, that's what she'd listen to — the sound. The words; who needs them? O well, onward.

An inevitable factor of growth is change. Growth is based on the assumption a change is desirable. Growing people are changing people. How can you know a changing person? Today he's different than yesterday and tomorrow different than today. You can't — no comfortable old worn tweed relationship. How can you base something worthwhile on the unknown? If you can't base a worthwhile relationship on a growing person — it must follow, growing people aren't worthwhile. Obviously static people are better people. People who never change are the only worthwhile ones — the only ones you can depend on to be always there, always the same. They never ask anything of you. They are nice.

Everybody wants acceptance, recognition, love... well I never had enough to mean anything. All I ever got from my relationships was the feeling that people weren't digging me as a thinking person. I never felt they knew or cared who or what I was; what they wanted from me was just my physical presence, just a body to warm themselves by and rattle every so now and then to let them know you're still there; how degrading can it get? I've been so lonely that just seeing a girl sitting way over on the guy's side when they drive by or a couple laughing together in a café made me

feel a terrific longing; I mean a real physical
pain — with me it burrows right in the pit of my
stomach and lays there like it was a rock — anxiety
— the fear and feeling that I'd never have a real
thing with a girl, but get this, at the same time I
knew I didn't want what they had. No, not one
affair or marriage in a thousand that has any real
significance any depth any warmth. Their sex...
habitual. Their life-pattern... routine. So I go on
hope-looking.

I love sleepyhead women and their tousled
early morning cat-stretching undrowsing.

One day... When our eyes have dimmed —
shrouded by time and tears — now dry. Worn... With
our quest for certainties on this — uncertain star.
Our thoughts, still young... We'll send weaving back
through the opaque and cloudy sea — of memories.
Look how... The fog of time all but obliterates our
conquests — now so diminutive. All but obliterates
our once so prided inanimate possessions, things we
gave our love for — so long unremembered. Now... rot
and rust. But there through the mist... There still
warm, there still live. The only certainty — in this
or any universe. Our perennial poignant... Love.
Darling, see... Our bodies aflame — in a phosphorescent
midnight sea... Then lovesleeping by an ember
fading, on the sandy edge of the world. A long ago
Christmas when we children kissed... and love was
born. Life's dawn, for eight squirming eager
puppies. To their mother, I a god — you a goddess...
and mine. Oh yes you were mine. The languid
luxurious Sunday-mornings way I urged you to
wakefulness — then you... wonderfully insatiable.
Each to the other we bestowed — now I know — life's
greatest gift. Wanting more... we chose negation.
The images began to obscure. How difficult to see...
Through a tear.

There is probably nothing more difficult
than re-evaluating something that has been with
you all your life, a thing that you have grown up
with, seen every day, accepted as commonplace,
attached no particular importance to. Now if this
thing also gives you pleasure and is associated
with something desirable and if this thing is also
a sexual symbol — there every day, the constant
aphrodisiac, you aren't going to *want* to re-evaluate
or acquire a new perspective. Naturally you'll cling
to the thing that's known, that's pleasurable... You
say there are so damned few pleasures anyway.

I knew she hadn't seen me sitting there in
the car, waiting for her. I just let her walk by,
just let her go on by without calling or touching
the horn. So great watching her walk: the way
her lovely ass moved, beckoning with each step
and those legs of hers, in sheer nylons they
looked nude and very tan tasty. She walked so
goddamned provocative in her four-inch heels,
kind of an elegant prance or like a thoroughbred
trotter — very proud. Some girls never seem to be
able to walk in heels, they always look as though
they're getting ready to squat — not her — Poetry —
dark legs flashing on those little stilts spelled
sex. Really, even after a year of marriage it was
still that way. Of course, as in her clothing, she
used impeccable taste in selecting shoes and they
did wild things for her. You know those long legs
were just about perfect anyway but when she gave
that elongated line to her calf through the
delicate little heel it was just too much. I can
imagine how many guys she must have driven nuts
every day... She looked like sex going somewhere to
happen and she was and I liked it.

Then a funny thing, while I'm watching
Sallee I see a girl coming in the opposite direction —
glance at her, look away but then I find myself

double-take staring. Something strange, different
about the kid. That's all she was: maybe fifteen/
sixteen, about five-four, wearing old worn-in Levis,
a boy's shirt, sandals of natural leather on her
feet. Her hair was dark and when it stirred with
her walking I saw reddish highlights, and it was
long, at least long for that time when the style was
all short cuts, bobs and the like — and straight,
just perfectly straight down past her shoulders.
Around her face it was cut in kind of a hit or miss
casual way, I suppose you'd call them bangs, anyway
it was nice the way it framed her face and it was a
good one — the face: really didn't show too much, she
was so young but what there was to show, she let
show. No pancake, no powder, good-sized mouth, full
sensual lips, no lipstick, she may have darkened her
lashes some — they seemed so full, but the eyebrows
were having more or less their own way.

The important thing to me — she was so
attractive, naturally attractive, and she looked
feminine as hell. There was absolutely no difficulty
in seeing this was girl... much girl, but with none
of the props I was so used to. What she was she
stated simply, quietly, with dignity — hmmm, yes,
dignity. She wasn't trying, you know? I watched her
down the sidewalk till she was out of sight, very
sorry to see her go — the way she moved in those
casual sandals so matter-of-factly and yet so
gracefully. There was kind of an animal litheness,
an animal readiness about her walk. She killed me.
I know now she was probably an escapee from New
York's Village or Frisco's North Beach or Hollywood's
Laurel Canyon.

Sallee was unhappy, bugged, not used to me or
any guy being gotten to by another girl when she
was there to be seen. I looked at her — looked at her
every so often driving home. When we got there I
went for a walk — thinking. Thinking about the girl

and Sallee, about the clothes she wore and Sallee's clothes, about her sandals and Sallee's heels. The way she walked, the way Sallee walked, and I suspected I was undergoing another metamorphosis — a re-evaluation of symbols and the "key" of the sex noises they made... Of shoes, of sandals that let a human walk naturally, functionally, beautifully, and little personal pedestals that force them to prance, look helpless, incapable of defense or flight — or often positively lethal in the game of sophisticated sex combat. Either way, this looks sensual to modern man! Yes, he wants his women helpless — conversely he appears strong, "Give me your arm darling, you'll trip on this rough street." Of course she'll trip, you idiot: those shoes weren't made for walking; they were made for posing, for showing off the calf, for enhancing the sex — whoreshoes, out-to-get-laid shoes — and they work. Either way, they do the job (functionalism is where you find it).

But what did they mean to me and to any guy who wants to take a *woman* to bed, a female who rejoices in, is content with, proud of, secure within, believes in her femaleness; has no need to carry a sandwich-board sign "Girl — Good Sex" or adorn herself with ad-agency-style gimmicks all intended to point up, enhance a thing that should never need this treatment. A thing for pride... To cherish, to keep pure and simple — and again, dignify.

You ask — is it important, really now is it worth all this dialogue? Listen! Some things I can ignore — not accept but ignore — but when our culture and its sinister fetishes distort the bodies of women, force most of them to walk as though they had poles up their asses, aborting their symmetry, displacing their internal organs, well things are getting out of hand.

44

The mind? Do you think anyone can totter around on those things — I don't care how competent they become at stilt-walking; do you think they can do this for one hour or ten and not get a mental reaction? Look! They are a physical manifestation of modern thinking within male/female relationships: "I'm only a girl, weak helpless dependent girl." The men love it and the women love it and I love it and hate it. I get sick and tired of shopping with girls whose feet are killing them. I want my woman able to get out of the way of a runaway cab. I want to want a female not a doll. The Chinese had this thing about female foot distortion enhancing femininity and now the Western world has this high heels thing. The physical distortion is ridiculous — yes but compared with the psychological it's insignificant. Imagine if you can the conditioning required to convince generations of men and women that the distorted calf is more beautiful than the natural.

You can't believe in distortion — in one distortion, without becoming more susceptible to the pseudo validity of other forms of distortion — mental or physical. Heels?... Yeah, they move me.

Our love's the same — yes infinitely wise. It knows the ephemeral quick beauty of... The flamboyant flame of sky at eve... Color-splashed exultant we kiss. Soft nocturnal rain, shared through a rhythmic windshield... In our small moving world... We touch. Those wild — or tender, ecstatic moments when you are my ultimate and I yours... Then into the dark... We whispering our love. A highway veers homeward — there the sudden Pacific panorama of Hermosa... And we awaken. Our weeping... Overwhelmed by the magnitude in the voice of our love — when first I spoke a poem... By the jetty by the sea. Come dearest one — your hand

to mine... So mixing our strengths — so transcending
our fear — let us follow for... Our love's the same.

But do you really have any idea of the
incredible beauty, natural functional beauty of the
human body? A fantastic work of Art — evolutionary
art. Yet I See that the mechanized extensions of
the human Mind and hand are also works of Art —
evolutionary Art. I've always had a natural affinity
for machinery; when I'm driving, I feel the
coordination of the machine's components, feel the
power-impulses from the combustion chamber through
the power-train to the road. And sometimes I feel
this thing when I'm walking; not often but
sometimes... This is when I'm alive. Not a consciousness
but that same natural affinity for functional
beauty, that same love for an efficiently designed
and built machine. If you feel this empathy with
functionalism — you may drive the machine hard,
factory-built or womb-built; you may give it hell,
push it to the max, but you will never ask it to do
what it cannot do. You are one with it... Precisely
attuned to its potentialities, its limitations.

And all the long days, I kept asking "Why
are we running?"

Music, a fever inside me, burning like crazy
always and no way out, no talent to tell my story,
sing my song, the need so great, caring not of no
talent — ruthless my need to sing, caring not for
inabilities, expanding in there deep inside,
feeding on itself, growing — it must speak, will
speak, caring not how it speaks, knowing only that
it must. And, yes, of course they laughed. Hell,
they should laugh; the boy must relate his little
tale, carve his initials into the bark of the world,
yes, good. But music? Ludicrous, really — aptitude,
ear, affinity? No. Nothing but need. The hard way,

impossible way. Why? So many other channels, so
many other trails and paths to follow all good all
gratifying but everything that was him, all the
health and sickness of him said sing. How well
remembered, the night I told Sallee I was leaving
her, leaving her because she stood between music
and myself, had no faith in me.

Imagine living with a man who refuses to
move in any direction save one and that direction
is blocked to him — a door deep in his unconscious
won't open, novor did, though he threw himself
against it, sometimes with a dogged desperate
frenzy. She never laughed, though I imagine she
must have cried, for my tragedy was hers and I left
my wife and it was the end of us and to this day
I'm sorry — Hell, yes I'm sorry, love is not cheap. I
knew hers was a real thing, but I felt — I knew,
she was pushing on the other side of that door, the
door I could open, but never would. (Sallee Music,
initials S.M., seemed appropriate to our relationship.)
Whether we had a chance or no I'm not sure but
music was definitely the out-front issue. I'd been
into it, singing and trying different instruments
since my teens. It was a passion and I just could
not get my talent together. She was not interested —
didn't believe I had it — wanted me in business —
some quick big money business. She liked music, but
she knew the people in it, friends of mine, and it
just wasn't solid and serious — all the drugs and
traveling and everybody broke. No, not for her
husband.

Now music is a thing of heart and guts and
balls and beauty — swelling with sex and hot and
cool with tenderness and calm — all these I had —
all these things I knew — but the door would not
open and each piece of lyric — each piece of melody —
each interval a new and different mind channel — a
slow process of piano to mind to voice — when this

was done — it all came crashing through — ripped out
of me — had been in there so long — pushing expanding
— a way — needing a way — not important the way —
being methodical-mechanical of no consequence — a
channel and it exploded — spewed out came at you
hit you hard — very hard — and so often there were
tears in their eyes — the door never opened — perhaps
my father had closed it long ago — closed and sealed
it — Freud, doctors or introspection never creaked a
hinge — but now there was a way — what matter its
slowness — inefficiency — the people never knew — the
agents never knew or cared — they loved it — I loved
it — Music and nothing else — One love and no other —
running for the wind — diet for the instrument —
feed it well — keep it strong — you need it for your
love — no time — no place for another...

So I split, left the beautiful thing to go do
my music thing... Set up a funky little studio in
my parents' backyard garage — a piano, the first
commercial tape machine, my super 2 bass, ten tom
drum kit which I built myself, helped to support
myself building drums and modifying drums for
other musicians. Began to play and sing and record
like mad — an intensity the like I couldn't have
imagined possible... Got better fast, got good and
then suddenly it happened. I was great! Mind blowing.
Formed a little combo, started gigging, toured up
into Montana, played a session at "The Doll House"
in Palm Springs, collecting fans everywhere.

The nights in dark smoky rooms, standing
alone in a white spot world, alone with my song...
my love. Yes, they loved my song — wanted to do
great things, big things for me, with me. Make
money for me, with me — "build me"... a little world
but a world mine at last, a place, yes. Each night I
burst out trembling with the intensity of the
thing, really — Larry Libido and his big fat hairy-
balled love notes. They trembled too, yes. The bass

player, "I don't know what you do in the last bars of 'Sorrento Man,' but like something happens up and down my spine. You're too much." Musicians, laymen, agents, friends and yes finally Sallee. Sallee, a weekend in Palm Springs, I'm working a club — she's there — I'm a pro — good money — nothing to stop me — can feed her at last — fame and adulation... For me? No, for us. Hang on baby, we're going up. I've got it made, we've got it made and it's a ball and I'm so sharp, so fucking sharp in my drapes and black shiny hair with the hard-to-work-right Tony Curtis hair lock falling front and the private world light lighting me, isolating me and with all that coolness thin over the passion and intensity, I killed her, literally killed her. "You're great Wulf — work great — look great — sound great — but I'm getting married." I went home and never sang again. I tried once later but couldn't. Didn't have any talent. Went into a stupor of stupidity limbo, of blah. Took me 3-4 years to come out of it. I'd always believed that a guy could have it all if he could pay the dues, work and work, keep on it and I did. But she was part of that "all" I would have, and she'd had it with the turbulent artist way of life. She got out of modeling, out of pictures into a stock kind of marriage and started having kids. Ah, normalcy.

This sad-sick story! Why bother? I've told it often and seldom anyone could feel the core of truth, the essence in the thing. The whole act was a residue of my early Robert Collier-styled religious training — the part that said, "If you want a thing, really want it, won't take no for an answer — man, go after it — you'll get it." Of course it works just as well for Frankenstiens or Madame Curies, grave robbers or charity workers — like each and all, psychological laws work for anyone who applies them whether they understand them or no.

I look at my life as composed of phases or eras and the eras are often remembered by the women who were there, and one-way-or-other important to me in that time. After Sallee I went through some serious bad times, kind of a numb depressed state and needed a serious change to pull out. This was the early 50's. I decided to make money and run with the fast set. So enter my Hollywood bookmaker era — and the women — mostly they were hookers. I mean I'd known love and had hopes but wasn't betting on it happening again. You had your choice; starlets, carhops, jitterbugs or hookers — the hookers were consistently the most attractive and uncomplicating. So the girls mostly were hookers. Much less with starlets who were pretty, beautiful but they were "career" crazy, working, always madly working on it, for it — acting class, voice class, the gym, dance class, auditions, vying trying to meet Mr. Madness. Carhops and jitterbugs didn't have the style — no time for feeling. No time really to get involved — that would come later. Emotionally they were on hold.

And in the deep — and I thought, never-ending — sad nostalgia for our lost childlove — I wrote my last-poems to her and she cried her last hurt — her requiem to our gone it's over time.

I stand on a deserted street... Alone, watching the iridescent glow of a taillight vanish in the night mist. The Finale — termination — end. Ten years of lover's chaos. Our theme... Erotica. Her theme... rules and convention... for she is chained. My theme — my doctrine — the wild nomadic wind of evolving Monastic rule... for I am free... That is why — with the night gloom and the still mist engulfing me... I weep.

50

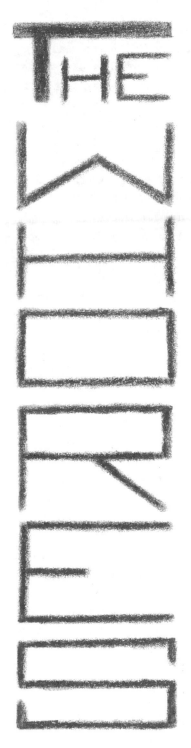

There they are... High up on the hill — they look down on the Strip, out over Hollywood, over cesspool L.A. — warm in their glass houses. There they are... sitting in Schwab's or Frascati's — warm with their sophistic world-wise talk and poolside-tan men. There they are... Racing down Sunset or La Cienega — warm in their glass and chrome success chariots... And they fuck, yes, professionally. They puff the sweet happy smoke through the minds of The Industry, blow clean the pipes and the psyches of the music people, the TV people, the picture people; the big people, the climbing people. One hundred dollars, or two or five. Busyness is success — no time for love — you hustle to get there and you hustle to stay and what's a C-note and a phone call to get laid and back to busy. And really, what else could she do with all her beauty? No — not stay in Kokomo and stagnate with the high school letter-sweater. No — not with fame and the call of seductive soft nights

and warm pools and palm trees and the beauty-boys
of the north and south and across the sea — all
waiting. Waiting with flash movie smiles and sharp
snarly Jaguar exhaust and her young hair wildfree
in the wind.

Drama class and dance class and sweat and fun
and love, so soon — how quick for beauty! Love so
sure and tall and lean and lithe and hard and hot
against her and the night sand still warm and
he smells clean and young and tastes of the sea
and she is all around him and he deep in her and
they are one flesh in joy and one joy in coming
and she thinks heaven is no longer a promise...
But she is wrong.

"No, honey, you know you can't, not back to
Kokomo — you'd go insane — the bit in the thing
they're shooting at Fox, they'll cast in two weeks —
it's yours. Listen, you're perfect for Loretta — go
read it for Max — he's looking for you and doesn't
know it, tell him I sent you. No, honey, not home,
not with your lovely little finger already curled
around it. Everything's breaking so well, don't be a
fool, another month and this town is yours... Stay.
Look, honey, you've never turned out, you're not a
hustler — just once — you need the time, you need the
money. Yes, really, five hundred for you, five
hundred for one who hasn't made the scene... one
like you."

And it was nice and he was good to her and he
was romantic even and he was tired and bored and
married and she gave him pleasure and stayed very
long and he was a star and she was impressed, his
name and face so large on the screen and in the
columns and touching him was like touching these
things and she was very good and he wanted to give
her more and she cried and tried not to go with the
money but she did, yes many times, yes many times —
but not for so much.

And she lay on her back and stood on her head, a circus with three Panamanian politicians, with little ships, with dildos, in hot soapy tubs of water and the sweet smell of pot and sometimes a fix and once a show with a Great Dane, for enough to pay off the mink.

And so she's a pro, lives high and her apartment is lush, a glass wall for her view and she loves, yes. And her love a desperate thing, so mad and wild, desperate we are together, trying with frenzy and tricks for the thing that's gone, the sweet tenderness that's gone, yes gone, yes, sold for a stinking five hundred.

Is it important or not, do they become stars or don't they? The ones I know who fucked to stay in town till something broke, and sexed their way up — they've lost the thing — that soft feminine thing, that yielding uncalculating trustful belief in men thing; what am I saying, lost it? Sold it. For what? To be in the movies.

But you know, it's amazing, really amazing how many kids in this town are hustlers. Sure I know they're all models or actresses, it's to laugh. I know one little girl whom I can't help liking, even had a thing for her when I first met her, she was so damned beautiful and her eyes threw such lovely green lights, when she looked. An empty-headed little pretty Pattie Lundeen is, and yet, she has a kind of pride and a sadness for her lost romanticism and a yearning for it. She says she's a model and drives an old Ford, lives in a tiny hillside apartment, likes to hang out with artists — you usually see her at Von's Café Galleria or The Unicorn or some such bohemian-style refuge, dresses casually, talking to some guy with long-hair-crazy or maybe a beard and paint-spattered pants and those green eyes so sad so pathetic it hurts me. Really, sometimes talking to this kid, feeling the

futility in her life, in her eyes, I feel her pain
inside me and it hurts... her pain does.

She still wants to use her sex in search of
love but of course she sells it, of course it's too
late, she's a whore, she fucks to eat, but just
enough to eat and put gas in her old fallapart
heap, that's all, no more. Just writing this I feel
so sad for her, so very sad... she's a nice kid.

If you had $80,000,000,000.05 you could buy an
airplane, or a boat, or a congressman, or a senator,
or a president, or a city, or a state, or a country,
or a war, or a whore-wife, or a movie star, or power,
or prestige, you could even buy a Cadillac, but you
couldn't buy an honest moment of friendship, or
love, or me.

Sure I've seen chicks with more symmetrical
faces, but her body says something, her face says
something — like I dig life — I dig love — Come! Love
me. When she moves to do anything, empty an ashtray,
cross the street — Everything! Her girl stomach,
her talking breasts, that articulate ass, say, Hey
man! Make it happen. Moving her lips, forming words,
she's really saying s-e-x. Why hell! Drinking, she
can't keep that wild tongue of hers from doing
interesting little things around the edge of the
glass.

Every move, gesture, declares and states her
theme — sensuality — It's crazy.

Well anyway, the first time I saw her was down
at Schwab's. I'd been working all morning on the
Jag, really looking beat, with grease and no shave.
I'm dialoguing with a cat about a transmission
problem, when I see her sitting down the counter. I
got a flash of those translucent green eyes and
something hit me, in the stomach — really — that's
the way some chicks get to me like there's a buzzsaw

going on in there till the thing is settled, one way or the other. I guess I'm pretty sensual too... Sybarite or satyr, call me what you will, I dig sex with a wild one and this one was the wildest. We got a thing going with the eyes, and man! She looked right at me — straight — no side glances, no lowered lashes, and those unbelievable green eyes said Yes. It was like the thing was spoken... It was spoken. The language we were talking, we could have communicated if she was an Eskimo and I was an Orangutan.

I said "later" to the guy I was talking with, and cut. While I was at the cashier paying my tab, she left her coffee and sandwich — still in good condition. We were both standing at the counter, not looking at each other, but standing close. I moved my leg, just a little — touching hers, pressing, just a little — and she quivered — the most lovely, responsive quiver you can imagine. Man! I just about came unglued.

I feasted on her, from her heels to the morning-after style hairdo, and said, "You're a tall one." She says, "I'm adjustable," and kicked off her shoes, picked 'em up, put her arm through mine, and we split.

I picked up her sandwich on the way. We sat in the Jag, and while we finished it off between us, we looked at each other — kept looking serious-like. It was real nice.

The car was running great, and I let her wind out in third, twisting up through Laurel Canyon. I was feeling so good I took a few at enough speed so that we got a little drift; it felt fine; I was driving good. I glanced over to see how she was taking it. She had one of those wonderful, relaxed smiles on her face — leaned over with her lips touching my ear, and said, "It's great to be able to know who a person is just by looking at their face.

Sometimes I make mistakes, but from the first it came through to me strong, there were no doubts — you just had to be you."

She put her hand on the back of my neck, the lobe of my ear between her teeth, then began playing around inside with the tip of her tongue. Who could drive? I shifted down — pulled the Jag off on that little side road behind Von's Café Galleria and we kissed. It was like coming — kissing her that first time — there sitting in the car. She melted into me so beautifully that I couldn't tell where I left off and she began. Really after Sallee it was the wildest feeling I've ever had — kissing. It seemed like we lost our identity, our separateness and kind of fused or melted into one.

We were so weak after, we just lay back in the seats, eyes closed, breathing very deep. Even thinking of that kiss now gives me chills. I'll tell you, I felt a little anxiety then. I wasn't sure I could handle her — that she might be too much for me.

She slipped her hand into mine, and with the warm and friendly way she moved her fingers through mine I knew that this was not just a ball — that she was people. And that, sex or no sex, I'd want to know her always.

"Sex is a waste of vital energy." — Lenin. And they liquidated the *Tsar!*

Diane worked as one of my phone girls during my bookmaking time. Sitting in a dingy room taking bets — paying for my tailored suits, my Cad convert, my house on Lookout Mountain Road. I guess I was father, lover, lots of things to her; she'd kind of kneel when I entered the room; I was the Good Book to her. I don't think I helped her much — more likely just fucked her up more — being easy to lean on — tough little mind though, perhaps if someday she stops selling her goodies, she'll swing... Perhaps. Funny how each new guy she holds up to me yardstick-style — flattering but really quite tiring. She's such a carnivorous one — a real peter-eater, virility-stomper, so 'course digs faggy guys. One day she could fall in love with her girlhood and begin a big fat phallic worship... Kneeling. Surrender herself to Yoni and become woman and let some guy, by her hair, off to his cave drag her, knowing she's surrendering nothing and gaining all of it.

The great tragedy of course in human beings: seeing so much, so far, and able to reach so little of it... tears us apart.

She was crying so quietly that through the sound of the soft October eve rain I would never have heard her in the traffic of that Paris night. I had stopped to light my last wick there in her Rue Pigalle doorway refuge, when I saw among the dancing shadows of the match flame the tired loveliness that was her face, a face that yet told her sad barter story, a face I recognized — she was on the street most nights. She had been walking in the rain and her tears lost themselves as they intermingled with the raindrops upon her cheeks, it was only the sound of her grief that had told me of its presence — and I knew it was the sound of a hopeless hope for love. In the diminishing glow of the match flame I offered her a hit. She nodded and smiling a smile of old old weariness, she turned her fingers so that I might see their wetness. I held the wick to her mouth. The form and movement of her lips, as she inhaled the smoke, touched me with their still soft, still feminine grace. We smoked it like that, silently watching the raindrops die in a sidewalk puddle, each forming

its own concentric ripples, only to be overwhelmed
by the dying of many more; and I knew her sorrow
too had died, for I could feel the now calmness of
her. Cupping her face in my hands, I held her eyes
a long moment. Slowly and very softly I touched her
lips to mine — her fingers on my arm tightened in
what seemed the most friendly and thankful
gesture I'd ever known. We moved out into the rain.
It felt good. She smiled that same weary smile and I
watched her go. Walking home, I found myself
hoping she'd somehow find her love. None waited for
me, I knew.

O how amoral is morality.

The beautiful Lincoln Continental and I, fast
wheeling down Laurel Canyon, metronome wipers
flicking away the storm. Driving, looking through
the rain always gives me a feeling of impending
drama, almost like in some motion pictures — first
they show you a provocative action shot like looking
through a windshield fast pushing through the
rain, then suddenly the titles come charging at you
right out of the picture with heavy music that fits
in, and that's what I was feeling — very alive,
excited — when I wet-streaked past a little drowned
rat of a girl limp-walking up the Canyon — and at
the first chance I U-turned and back, pulled up
beside her, pushed open the door — "get in." "I'm all
wet." "So!" And on my hearth we build a fire and she
tells me she's not caught in the storm, she likes
walking in it; and she's kind of earthy-real and
she talks of her life and her tyrannical husband
and of her polio and beautiful-face artist modeling
and "If we make love I can't be with you again,
can't be your friend and I do want to be — really —
really I do." "Now is now, tomorrow is what?" We're
sitting watching the fire and the phone rings.

While I'm standing talking I keep looking at her —
easy at first and she looking back easy — then
suddenly we're looking hard — very — and I hang up
and give her my hand — she followed into the bedroom,
our fingers touching —
    ah the kiss was young
     eager, alive and wanting
      ah the kiss was old
       the eternal rhyme
       old as time
        and the soft of her mouth
         moved against mine
         and the smooth of her tongue
        moved against mine
        and the need of her body
        moved against mine
        ah the kiss was young
         eager alive and wanting
        ah the kiss was old
         the eternal rhyme — old as time
         the eternal rhyme...
and all intertwined — and on the bed holding close —
and kissing her ears and neck and shoulders and
breasts and with her fingers touching my cheek
she stopped me at her waist — "No, inside me hurry
please" — And moan-whispering "I am, I am, oh yes,
yes, yes, oh yes it's been so long" — over and over
she kept saying this but quieter and quieter till
it's like a purr — Now her face is good, so very good
to see, so soft and still, now she is pure — in her
face I see all through her, what is on her face is
inside and inside she is what is on her face — a
single clear note, of one color, one substance, one
with the earth and with all growing things and
the wind and the sea — she is this, she is my love
and my love is forever with purity, and gone dying
in the unpure.

I looked out of the window — my god, what a
rain — heavy — she rose and went into the bathroom;
I heard the shower run... Watched her soap herself-
-enjoying it. "I told you if we made love I couldn't
see you again, remember." "Look girl! Today is
beautiful — the storm, meeting you; you worry about
tomorrow, I feel too alive to be concerned for it.
The moment is good, I ask nothing more. The storm
gave you — I give you back."

Standing by the door watching the drumming,
gurgling, hissing, straight-falling water, with the
fire crackling at our backs, she said "No I'll walk,
I love the rain."

She of the rain, clean as the rain, I watched
her down the turning stone stairs to the street —
suddenly shouting Wait — stay — I ran to her,
breathless. Standing there in the middle of the
street looking at each other solemnly and with the
torrent through our hair, streaming over our faces,
blurring the vision of each other we kissed —
wonderful kissing lost in the storm, with the
mouth-tastes of each other all mixed with the rain-
taste. She turned in my arms, her eyes held mine
for a moment, the touch of a smile and she was
gone.

Standing in the middle of the street, coatless,
hatless, wet to my soul, god I felt alone watching
her go — stood till the falling homeward sea
obliterated her. She and her little limp were gone —
gone to her tyrant and his loveless house.

My rooms were full of the smell of her, and
empty — I couldn't stay and drove down through the
rain feeling heavy, with a kind of sadness for all
us hungry creatures.

I know this thing I'd love to have for myself —
the ability to esthetically appreciate her physical
beauty without feeling compelled to possess it. How

many times in my life have I knelt before beauty,
played rug for a wild-looking thing. Yes, I'd love
having one around, a lovely one; but please, no
more, not the incredible compromise of accepting
boredom — accepting for a happy eye and bogging
down the brain.

I can't really categorize hustlers. Most
marriages are just a low-level opportunistic hustle.
Man — if you sell it, you sell it.

Going past the market on the street to her
house the deep red plums flashbacked me to Sunday
and our after-surf swim eating a dollar's worth of
the damn things, being the favored flavor of her
and lips the same deep red and me stained all over
of lips and favored flavor and then child-vowed
forever loves and now bought new dollar's worth of
deep red favored flavor and now remembering, and
now running fast faster and the joyous promise, the
other phone bell tinkling... and deep red crushed
lips saying "Oh! I'm busy."

What more can I give you? With me you may be
you — wholly you — draw no lines, plant no markers —
taste the pinnacles, the chasms of earth and flesh —
much much much too much freedom. Your lost-child
eyes asking please — right or left me, good or bad
me, show me show me show me — please don't, not free —
decisions, never could really make them, such
lonely things — what do you think I should wear —
these earrings, are they right with this — go to
Rome, well I don't know, what do you think? Me? I
think you're all marshmallow inside — I think you
want me for daddy — hell with you, I've got a
daughter — want a woman female she-animal so I may
give her my male for her fe - - - -

I see it whenever and wherever — girl, love
your strength no less no more than mine — come

complete, you and I — understanding — it moves into
your eyes, your smile, your body — give me your
hand, come share a daylife with me... dream dust.

I can still smell her. How sweet, how
mysterious, how very — like nothing you could ever
feel or hold or know or love or... like a thing from
the unknown, a lifeless another world. Woman,
human animal, female — the conceiving counterpart
of male? Yes — then why the mystery, the unknown?

Animal — why not an animal smell... why? Hell,
it would terrify the world... yes.

Who? Who would want to lay her? Only another
animal — some simple being with his feet in the mud,
the soil, the earth — and his hands on the stars...
yes.

Only him. He looks too wild, he looks too free,
he could kill on impulse — or love — and for no gain
and for the moment and for the need unpremeditated,
uncalculated, mutual, honest. Self-scented sex... yes.

Self-scented — yes, a flower's scent is lovely,
as is man's — both beautiful, both of the same, and
not the same. It is good.

How strange people are in the routes they take
for pleasure, their futile chasing after a...
They've even forgotten what they were after when
they started the chasing running thing long ago,
forgotten what they were asking for, running after;
so incredibly unknowing... Yes. Money, games —
sometimes they do well; but living! They are
completely out of it, their trying sometimes is kind
of funny, maybe if you're not hurting too much at
the time it's funny.

So like these two chicks got a call from the
she-pimp-spider in her glass web hanging over
Sunset who never balled for bread herself but with
a phone and a book of numbers and a reputation,

62

and being around so long she was swinging loaded —
'times the spider could even looking down see the
glint-sun swimming pool at the pad where her little
chicklets were breeding up her bread. I don't
really put her scene down, at least not hard. "The
spider" is a coinage of Diane's or probably more like
Betty's. Well anyway, the two hustlers go to this
guy's pad and he opens the door, takes them into the
bathroom, asks them to get nude, fills the tub with
hot water, peels the butcher-smell paper off a nice
fat roasting-poultry-type cleaned and plucked
chicken — off the clothes, into the tub, chicken
under his arm like he's going for an end run or
some kind of a football bit; chicks, the pros that
they were, playing it straight — half a yard apiece
you know, cool and straight — "All right girls, this
is what we do," and now he's beginning to fondle
the bird, loving it up quite a bit — "What I want is
for you to yell and keep yelling," and by now the
cat is obviously horny as hell and he's breathing
pretty fast and a big hard-on and he jams the
rooster's hole over his pecker and starts pumping
and yelling "Fuck that chicken" and pumping and
yelling "Fuck that chicken, c'mon girls yell fuck
that chicken, fuck that chicken" — they're yelling
in unison, being pros, and the cat's really flipping
and the girls keep yelling "Fuck that chicken" and
he does and he makes it, and the plucked one is a
fucked one; and the girls, having their money, dress
and split... Wonderful.

Or how about the one Betty Moore tells me — the
same scene — she goes out to turn-one and when the
"john" answers the door it's very weird, like the
cat's completely without clothing except for a tall
old-time-style silk hat and strange perhaps pirate-
type boots, the kind that roll over at the top like
in the movies, and a little whip in his hand. Well,
being unshakable, having made lots of routes, well

really more 'cause she's so damned volcanic inside
if she ever... Well, you know — anyway she doesn't
ruffle a hair in an eyebrow, asks his name, he
affirms, invites her in. It seems he comes on like
this so that if it shakes the girl when he opens
the door looking so far out and all, he passes
'cause he wants an all-out swinger, no other. She
said he didn't get too rank though. She worked over
his cock and balls with the little silk whip, he
beats her ass some and balled her there; it's all a
little strange isn't it — "A little strange!!!!"

Which explains why you see quite a few
hustlers around who are pushing forty. You look at
them, wondering how they're making it. "You wouldn't
want to make-it with them." Well, that's the story:
experience — twenty years of every conceivable kind
of balling, every conceivable kind of deviation.
Hell man, they're teachers now — they don't turn
them, they learn them.

    Soon you'll be dead, you know, it will be done
    Soon you'll be dead, you know, and it will be
done
    Yes, done
    Yes
    Did you smell the blossoms on that orange tree
you pass every day —
    Did you kneel and look into the eyes of the
little child and with your fingers touch the
softness of his hair —
    Did your mouth taste the sweet ripeness of
pink melon, and did you feel its life become yours —
    Did you move your skin against that of your
love and feel the response that says — that always
says, eloquently says... yes yes you live.
    Soon you'll be dead, you know
    Who knows, perhaps something someone
somewhere is beginning a fire

Who knows, perhaps something someone somewhere
is beginning a rain
    And the burning and the raining will be into
eternity.
    See —
    As you sit and the cities burn behind you and
the waters rise round you,
    Your tears only add to its strength...
    Yes, cry —
    Yes I am crying now — for you — for you — I cry
    You never smelled the blossoms or looked into
the eyes of the child
    or were loved —
    Or loved —
    You never lived —
    You never did, did you?
    I remember your saying, "I will soon — soon
when there's time —
    I only have three more payments to make."
    You'll soon be, dead, you know

    Look, you're dripping blood
    on your glisten and chrome machines
    on the thick soft floors of your sterile rooms
    In the body-warm water of your swimming pools
    I see it hang bright red for a moment,
then lose itself in the chlorine.
    My blood too is spending — runs the length of
my fingers, hangs suspended a moment, then goes to
the earth, and becomes itself again.
    Yes, we are all bleeding
    Dying
    Bleeding
    Dying
    How many drops have you —
    Have I —
    There is no count —
    Can't be counted —

Never — never
Urgency
Yes!
There is urgency —
Not to motion, not to prestige accomplishment,
not to acquisition —
No — no
To the clean sea on your skin
To life-giving sun warming you through
Through to the earth —
The brush of velvet lips upon yours, and upon
your ecstasy
Come back —
Come back —
Here, take my hand
And, yes, I'll take yours.
Our need is great
Mine of you, yours of me
Come — here! Lie by me in the green, soft grass
Isn't the tree beautiful — isn't the tree lovely
And see how nicely it filters the sun when we
ask it to cool us
Look at the woodpecker, how funny, how
seriously he works —
Oh! I like the way you laugh. Good to laugh
together.
Forget about the payments — let them take it
back — we'll walk —
we'll walk again
How much better
So much better —
Remember what lovely things happened walking —
The painter — the young one — he was good with
watercolor.
He told us of Paris, his eyes asked for
friendship.
You still have the painting.
The small puppy — happy leaps — remember, he

kept bringing that stick to throw, and followed
us...
God he was beautiful! — as you.
And those rocks, those great free-forms, by the
sea and the moods they gave me — for sculptures
Soon you'll be dead, you know...
She read my latest writing and said it was
savage
I said, someone has to say it.
I touched her and she whispered, I must go.
I said, but your sex is your life, I know, once
I saw it in your eyes.
How can you go — how can you sell your love.
She said I know, but only three more payments
Not everyone has a pink Thunderbird.
It's very foolish. I saw a thunderbird once,
and he was brown — brown and graceful flying. I
liked him.
I said, but you loved me
— I know
Christ, girl! Everyone can see it — They've
never seen you so alive as with me
She said Yes I know, I know, I'll always love
you —
Only with you I live —
But where are you going? With your words and
your song
Ah she knew me, she read the thought in my
eyes — I saw the grief twist her face — it was very
quick, no one must see
I loved her — it tore a sob from me —
She laughed at my empathy — they may have been
watching
Soon you'll be dead, you know —
Yes, soon
Perhaps if you could see the blood, the way
it's smeared and smeared over your pretty things —
In the glass, on your dress heels, I could

see it —

You couldn't, could you?

I could see it — and the face of your true love reflected there — and the death of your sex — Remember, you sold it.

No, I don't believe my writing is savage.

But, yes, sometimes I understand your fears of it.

Ah you come to me in pain, and I help to cleanse the wounds, and you help me with mine —

You come to me in Joy — with a thing of beauty — in your hand or in your mind — and hold it out for me to share like a happy child.

And your joy becomes mine and I a happy child and yes, together we lay on our backs and watch the clouds cross our sky and we laugh and show each other the everchanging animals and faces and valleys and hills, and we laugh —

It's very good.

If you or I should turn on our stomach and cry That's good too —

In a way —

My grief is yours and yours mine

My love is yours and yours mine

And hate and fear are things that can be shared too —

All right, what are you trying to say, to say with your critique, with your leaving —

This going back — this joining hands with — this ring-round-rosy with the idiots' scene.

These are your words:

I'm sick — doing horrible things with grotesque people — for things. I'm so bland and insipid and afraid and filled with rot.

I don't want you to see me that way. I can't subject you to the person I am — Really, you wouldn't believe the things I'm capable of for things.

Stop the babbling.

Yes, I know —
I must know.
These same things are eating my insides —
Now
At this very moment
Gnawing at me —
Do you think you are a goddess —
Do you think I'm a god —
We're pitiful human animals spawned in a
putrid culture, malignant
   With corruption conditioning —
   Only the few — the gutty ones, yes, the
courageous ones
   Pitting the minds, the reasoning against the
monstrous lie that says life is a pittance and
things are the essence
   My god, dear one, why do you desert me —
   Why are you leaving me
   Gently sometimes you touch my arm — kiss my
cheek — my lips,
   Turn and walk away.

THE Out bar-flitting, Wilshire to Hollywood, watching the lushes and tight glued-on pants, dry-coitus cha cha wiggle each other to orgiastic tenor players' Elvis-like gymnastic cha cha blowing — getting beer-horny and knowing I won't get laid, that all this shit is over for me. Making wet-glass circles on the bar, pensive reminiscing, and comes back to me; one late-early coffee shop and yes — her lone surly eyes sparking yes — that mutual spontaneous animals-in-heat so-seldom thing, having nothing to do with love but unrationally magnificent in release — from way back in some black cave came her need-primed one-purpose supple body smacked against me, hating clawing kicking biting — my hands rough bruising brutal, and me all obscene in her hair, between her breasts, smearing all over and up her and she groaning and yessing, dirty mean and low — he-she-cat clawing digging, teeth slashing — cervix-deep in hot slippery gushing pounding leg-locked frenzy — my writhing back, whiplash red crisscrosses fingernail-furrowed dripping — and when we start, her face wide-eyed twisting insane, and sink my teeth in her neck, taste-mix sweat-blood, and my life spastic pours into her... And we death-sleep unmoving hours, and waking too big and close to

FAGGOTS

understand, and reverent awe, monosyllable-mute,
part nameless.

Trance staring slowly back in focus at drying
circles on a formica phony-wood bar top — think...
This futile insipid bar-sex with working to get 'em
drunker, to get 'em in the car, in my place... In.

'Times her hurting hunting eyes talk to me
from down the bar; but why? Only another scene, and
after you've been laid — really, that pelvic-palaver
masturbation is more draggy than the onanistic type,
which 'times is a gas — like any mutual coming this
side of important-passion-cohabitating is better
passed; and do-it-yourself is as good... And the same
solution anyhoo.

Anyway the last bar stop was the corner of
the Canyon and Sunset, the Lauralite, where I'd
talked myself in and out of more than any other in
all those Hollywood years, and has usually a good
portion of hustler-starlets, looking like they want
it very much... Wondering what *it* is. And ninety-
some pounds of quite cute blond saying she'd dug me
since about a year ago when Don Chastain introduced
us — I don't remember her, and say "Let's split" and
we goodnight Joele, her new friend and my old
friend — first French-girl love and walking down
Sunset to that little pet shop past Fairfax, I see
how very good she is by how she nose-to-glass looks
and talks to the hang-tailed monkeys and sleep-
flea-scratching poodle-baby — and her really quite
cute little profile, and how talking, sitting on a
Strip bus-stop bench, I understand, tho she doesn't
say this — she very gutty helped her cancer-devoured
father from his poor wounded flesh. And I "Sweet
thing, step into Rand's 'All you can eat for $1.75'
doorway and I'll kiss you" and we did, nicely, and
funny people after eating busting out, mashing us
together with flung door and all laughing — and
back behind the Lauralite kissing in the car, it's

nice, no passion, but we still really like each
other and don't stupid try to build what isn't, if
we're to have a time this is not it, but friends —
yes.

Back at the Lauralite for Teddy, my practically
professional-status bar-hop-fly evening's companion,
and he back-slapping "D'ja get lucky, dad?" With him
so lush-loaded, no point in telling him she was
people, so I drive his drunken self homeward and
he — "Man, if I don't make some kind of a scene, I'm
in a bad way;" he wants to make it with me, and
smaller eyes I couldn't have if I'd just finished
Brigitte Bardot — and "this" very ordinary, very
everyday. I have few close male friends who at one
time or another haven't given me the homo-sign: that
affectionate affected fag falsetto, a drunken pat
on the ass, that leering lewd double entendre
girl talk, but mostly almost indiscernible — with
being buried so deep in a big pile of old unfaced
unresolved questions and hang-ups, smolder-
festering somewhere in the unconscious, and all of
it straight out of million-years-old unisexed or
hermaphrodited or whatever past, or since-birth-
learned genital jealousy or mirror-digging
narcissism, but it's there and forever rooted deep —
and I understand much of my father's hostility
to me.

Yes, deep and ubiquitous, some understood by
the cool read-everything enlightened ones — guilt-
tinged, suspected by most. And psychopathic terror
shredding suspected by slug-riddled public-enemy-
number-one, fast-running from self, police thirty-
eight-splattered, flip-flop broken boneless sprawled
catsup-covered meat, lone-hate-dying on a strange
cold sidewalk slab, far from the "Mother" that
whimper pink-bubble froths on his poor last breath...
And great ruthless God, why? If it's stock standard
equipment on all hes and shes, why hush-hush and

Freud and Kinsey "only interesting" — and facts are things we don't build our movie-set lives on, our quick-as-a-sunset phffffffffft it's over lives, dear ones. Who has time to play games to decorum?

And my father, ogre-tall, finger-wagging, "If I catch you playing with that thing again, I'll cut it off."

Not this one — when I lust, I take it out, that lust from where they told me I should keep bad never-never things, and if it says not hurt but good for loved ones or self (same thing) then it may have me if it will — my lust. And that robust, practical-minded kid I remember from school — "Jerkinoff? — Shit, it's mine, isn't it"... Great — but they are so few. Most so tender-young-fragile, easily stuffed, shoehorned into molds and there spend slow dragging "What was it all about?" lives, crimpcramped in and out of animal shape... O my! Such dreary dreary sadness — though it's mostly more true in bright, shiny God-bless-it (did he?) America. What can you say of the homosexuality problem? Other than it does not exist — like, say, the Jewish or black problem or claustrophobia cease to exist in the clean white light of — Why? Curious all-accepting all-questioning Why? The answer to Bubonic Plague and the Milky Way and your swish-hipped, lisping, lilting faggotry.

I'd like a jar of Instant Mother's Milk please.

Dykes pansies queers butches swishes fairies queens aunties and all; and psychiatrists tell 'em to adjust — how do you adjust to an eccentric out-of-round social wheel — it's always going to be rough — you can learn to move with it some but it's going to shake you up as long as you ride — so to hell with the shrinks — we need a new wheel.

Heaven and reincarnation and any of that: if it's true and it does happen... Crazy! Long spiraling ascending gold gleaming stairs, harp singing gate and all the chicks in white Grecian gowns... I'll buy — or perhaps as a black panther sixty mile an hour muscle-flowing across a jungle clearing neuroticless killing... Yes. But not on hearsay... No. No, for that my microscopic eye has no eyes, and when I catch the worm's eye, it's over. Anyway, so much more of an earth-angel am I than they; my ticket should be valid — that is if there's someone there to punch it. Gimme another toke.

Now don't cry. Don't cry. You want Mommy and Daddy to be proud of you, don't you?

Afraid? You're damn well right I'm afraid. The thing spreads — I used to think they were all faggots, they've gotten so far from their animal maleness. But now I know they're neuters — anal. I'm watching it spread over the world. If there were a hope, myself and others like me would be that hope — if there were.

The biggest fattest most obnoxious aggressive businessmen are constantly cigar-sucking and chewing — the more successful, the bigger they suck — oh my!

Diane and I had gone to Von's for coffee. Great sitting outside at the little tables in the sun, and there a character at another table with coffee and a Chihuahua pup on a leash. The little thing quivered all the time, just kept shaking, not cold — nervous. I'm a guy who prefers relaxed animals, people or pets, so this fur-bag of raw nerves has no attraction: Diane, being the silly bitch she is, had to babytalk and pick up the little vibrating machine. The guy on the other end of the leash was Johnny.

He called the dog Diz. We told him to drop in (it turned out he lived across the street from Lynn and her). When we left, he winked at me. I say to Diane, "Who needs a faggot with a Chihuahua?" The next thing I know, he's found a home. Every time I stop to see the girls, he's there.

Let's face it — people in general don't accept me. They're sure I'm not for real. A little too strong for the norm's sensitive stomach I'm told. Not Johnny, he's 19 and read everything he could get his hands on, understood some, and a good fix on most of the writers; a very intelligent one, and a hell of a good friend. His thoughts, conclusions were beautiful — a joy watching his mind work. And it always is, must be, in any creative relationship, we helped one another immeasurable. With his level of understanding, rather than shy away as soon as he found that I demanded he level, be honest, he had a ball purging himself. He knew I'd understand, only interested — yes, no censor, only interested. If I said a thing was idiotic, instead of fumbling to the defensive... "Why?"... Must be the most beautiful word of all, "Why?" — not with antagonism, defensively, with phony hung-up pride — no, just a flat, curious, wonderful "Why?" The healthy ones I've met why everything — introspectively, objectively.

The way he acted the day we met? The clowns! I mean — how can one man when he feels the sheer weight of their mass against himself — 1,000 to 1 — 10,000 to 1 — 1,000,000 to 1 — who knows — I mean — you have to be a very strong one not to be impressed, dominated, coerced by their very numbers and don the indicated harlequin cap, and you're a clown in a club — and Johnny's was his latent fagness.

Hell, I walked down Wilshire Boulevard in the hot middle of a July and there they were, 12:00 noon — uncaged for their hour, and almost to a man, in dripping white shirt, tie, French cuffs, soggy

suit, even a vest, and all sweltering. (No, some
don't perspire — a phenomenon of the living dead.
These guys aren't men, aren't faggots — they're
neuters.) I'm no-shirt and denims, and because of
the minority-majority thing, bohemian-square thing,
I feel a twinge of guilt, self-consciousness — they
are right, I'm wrong. I throw it off with a roar —
really. And this 90°-in-the-shade, tight-collar-and-
tie type's illogical, unreasoning, conformistic
attitude motivates everything, every move they make
— neuterism — they're saturated with it. One drop,
one little drop of this asexual conformity and I
throw it off like the malignancy it is.

    Johnny and I driving past a chic women's
shop with this mannequin in the window. "She looks
like the girl we were just talking to," and she did
— if you put that girl in there behind the glass
you couldn't have told the difference. Actually
there really wasn't any. Funny thought. These
window mannequins are so highly stylized, girls
follow along, copy the make-up, hair-style, as well
as the clothing they show.

    By the time I realized I wanted to have sex
with my mother, she was too old and fat.

    These are statements human being to another,
sometimes in torment, sometimes in glee, sometimes
high on an ego-jag, but always trying to get the
Truth of it. I think I know as I lay on that
ridiculous analyst's couch, writhing, panting,
sweating, that it was not the way, not in the quiet
damp emotion-steamed darkness of his womb-room. No —
out in life, mixing it up, exposing myself, exposing
others, experimenting with my fears and theirs —
there was the laboratory, the dissecting room — out
there in the world... World of people, hot-cold, wet-

dry people. If there was to be an answer or answers, that is where they lay. And timid-bold, that is where I went... where I go. I had asked the Freudian one, the Jungian one, the classical one, the iconoclastic one, whoever, whatever he was, I never did really know. "Am I gay, a sweet faggot, is my virility a lie for daddy... Or true? Can you help?" But no, it's a self-service life — perhaps you pay on the way out, who knows? But for now, kiddies, if you're hung up, you must unhang yourself or stay hung. 'Cause really — no one really cares but you... Really. So I went out alone to suck my first cock, and it was good, as sex is good; and each time since, it was good, as sex is good; and I can feel love for a boy; and I have. Romance — no!

And sex, sans romance is without the True wings of ecstasy... And only the movement of her body brings me to longing... And only the movement of her body lifts me in wanting.

You've never loved anyone? "No." The dog, you love him. "Yes." Your not loving is a way of saying you hate sham — falsification — superficiality. The dog is clean, pure, you can love him — you've never found anyone except him worthy of your love. To me, this is great, beautiful. Don't you realize what this says? What great strength you have? The best or nothing, the clean or nothing, the pure or nothing.

Who are you to put anybody down? I'm the greatest man alive — aren't you?

Suggestion to distilleries: Package bourbon in baby bottles with nipples. Don't be afraid. Go ahead. You'll rule the world.
Suggestion to cigarette manufacturers: Make your filter tips the color and shape of breast nipples — the suckling should increase immeasurably.

Later, in Paris, can-can dancer Celine in her
constantly charming French-garbled English would
say, "I doon understand you making love to the boys-
-you doon act like that." "You mean I'm not swish,
don't act gay?" I'm not — certainly not homosexual,
not heterosexual, not bisexual. I'm sexual, sensual,
believe in touching, believe in physical love, in
demonstrative love. If I feel to kiss or caress or
suck or fuck a friend, I do it, to be as close as
possible, to give or take whatever tenderness or
violence lies there innate in the relationship... I
mean who made the rules?

And all the long days I kept asking — where's
the masquerade?

And I don't really know about faggots. I've
seldom had a discussion with them where we get
past the information on the dust cover, maybe it's
my fault, but sometimes the gay-ness seems like
sadness — and of course the very fact of their
homosexuality is a vaginal denial — denying the
vagina, you deny your source, and thereby yourself;
and into this impossible paradox any fairly adjusted
overt homo has twisted the frame of his days. I'm
not talking of kids who question the thing, who
possibly understand a little the insane life-
rejecting death-wish inherent in that kind of an
existence, who realize their pathology and go out
in life to get back to vagina and pursuit of same,
to become homosapiens, ex-homosexual. I sure as hell
would never want sex that way again. You've got to
be a highly evolved human being to give or get any
but superficial pleasure in mating; and life is
much too complex and sometimes even too much fun...
for games.

Levis, no shirt, sun-black — I'm swinging
barefoot down Laurel Canyon; and it wasn't the
first time I'd seen her, lots of guys in the Canyon
had too — she lived just up the street. We'd talked
of her, were woman-curious... yes woman, not girl.
This was woman walking towards me up the hill,
her sweet-voiced children chattering French and
she, rich female-voice that rubbed along my
sensuality... it always did. I friendly hi'ed her,
and she noncommittally hello'ed and we just stood
for a little, kind of adding each other, and her
eyes were grey — with all the rest of her and grey
eyes, and I felt myself going to her even then.

I said "beautiful" and with loose expansive
flung arm take in the whole canyon, with all its
green, and bird, and tree, and peace, and sun,
and sky-ness, and her.

She yes'ed noncommittally.

I leaned to her, inhaling, "You've got to be
kidding; perfume? On an insane-smelling day like
this," and grabbed beside the road a fist-full of
wild pungent posies, stuck them in her face, "There!
Real perfume! You're violating the day and yourself."
And barefooted on down the Canyon and didn't see
her again for about a week, and then I brought
another bundle of wildflowers for her, and she
invited me and we sat in the garden where I told
her I wanted to make love to her, and she
noncommittal. Each time we talked in the garden she

ALIANNE

told of her life, of France in war-time, and Nazis, and her war-raped child body, and her underground resistance fighting — and dancing ballet and chorus-line after the war, and then a ridiculous Can-Can gig at Latin Quarter New York, and tiring of showgirl life and wanting security and family and married a small love.

And a day at the beach, though I'd never spoken again other than tone and eyes — lying in the sand, turning to me sudden-like in French-honeyed-English "I could not sleep last night because I want you so much, so much I want you" — and all so lush and rich with female-sexed overtones, and with her body and passion she drenched me, she draped her living womb over me, and through each portal of ethereal and carnal expression she dragged me, into a hot-scented-thick-woman-juiced cocoon, and I emerged a new-born... left the boy behind.

All images on the retina of the eye are upside down... and perhaps — I think: the Devil is really God, and God the Devil.

She said "Please. O yes, you must tell me, let me know if I am too heavy on you. You see you can now hurt me very much, but if I am understanding you, I will not press and be heavy on you, then perhaps I will not lose you — you are my love." Sweet Truth, just thinking about her naturalness, her grace and these in sex so beautifully essential to me. I said "You were lovely, I think of it so often. It feels just marvelous."

She said "Darling I have arranged it, we can spend a day together — one each week, there is someone to see after the children. You can write, we will make love, you can write, we will make love"... "Yes." I love saying yes to her — we laughed. Our joy a little solemn — very romantic together, strange is this stayed with us — the strong romantic feeling. Don't worry please, you won't become too heavy on me, I'll be honest, let you see me, what's happening inside — what I want. If I can be really honest, perhaps there'll be understanding. No pain! O that would be nice — no pain. Not possible of course. We know of the inherent pain in joy — ours no different — let's expect the pain, it will come you know, o yes it'll come ripping through us, you and I... It must be so — children — playing games with our lives. Our beautiful instincts, trying to bend them to fit some pattern they can understand. How could they? The pattern's not real — exists nowhere in reality — only in some monstrous ideology. Social coercion — distorted molds — we press us into these. Another sweet promise is lost... lost again.

Most scenes I witness look like a film clip from a movie. The acting is always good, though.

What's his story? Since I told him I was going to Paris, he's been staying away; and when he does come around, he stands on one foot, then the other, mutters some inane crap, and when I look up, he's gone. Alianne says he might be jealous, hurt that I'm leaving, cutting his dependency. Hell — I don't want to run a class, play daddy — *I want comradeship — communication — love.* These I can't have from immature ones. Wonderful if he gained strength from me, and if part of his strength was of me he'd feel closer, much closer than before; and if he stood tall, free, a self-reliant, self-loving human being, the friendship would be worth so much more to me. So he's only 21. So? Forget the chronology. A man or woman is mature when they're mature — not before — not later — not at 15, 40, or 80 — wisdom, maturity is where you find it. Some of the greatest idiots I've met were proud of their longevity.

Everyone is a many-faceted schizophrenic—but you can't love them for the sides that don't reflect the light. A thing is good as long as it's good, no longer; a thing is bad as long as it's bad, no longer. If I've learned anything in this life, and the learning of this is one of the toughest—if they want to go, let 'em go. If a thing isn't mutual, mutually gratifying, it's not alive—it stinks, like all dead things. And there's no life in a one-sided love. Like artificial respiration: only a fool keeps working after the body is cold. Of course you hate to see a loved one go—I know. You want to plead—beg—reason—logic. Forget it—you can't reach into their minds and shift gears, rearrange things, push back the blocks and barriers. Really, the worth of a relationship is in direct proportion to the honesty practiced within that relationship. You look at it as though people function in different strata of integrity or truthfulness. If you attempt to become intimate with those on a lower stratum, you'll always be attempting to pull them up to your level, can't help it. Their defense mechanisms, subterfuges, devices, lies, conscious or unconscious, are quite obvious; and this constant pulling up, interrogating, is tiring, very tiring emotionally, very boring, and obviously leaves no alternative than to reject them. With Johnny the relationship was significant only because he more closely approached my level of perceptive frankness. But carrying my emotional load and his too, being my conscience and his too, evaluating the psychological ramifications of my acts and his too—let's face it, I have my own load to carry. I or no one else has the strength to carry another very far. I would have to stop, and I have no intention of stopping. If someone wants to walk along, or help, lead and be led—great—crazy—nothing in this whole world I want more. He picked me to emulate—but so have others. I've had it with that one, I'm ready for a new scene. "You're great. Let me kneel at your feet, walk in your shadow." "Yes it's true, I'm great. And naturally such awareness manifests itself in love for me." O come now, Wulf, please! The offering of love in itself is of no significance. The ones who love strength, just strength — strength that springs from any source, the pose of strength, assumed attitude of strength — the life actor, of those that love courage — just courage — can they differentiate between the fantastically rigorous, social-disciplined courage of the terrified soldier charging meat-chopping machine guns because someone blew a whistle... or the trembling tear-cheeked courage of the boy who in the quiet of the night climbs from his window, leaving an impossible home life to go alone into the world? No they can't - - never. To them, the pose, attitude, stance of strength and courage is enough, and even if you stand tall and hollow they'll cling to you with all they have.

Trouble is, all the baddies have goodie smiles.

"I love you, je t'aime, mon amour you are my life, a day without you is not a day. I love you — I love you — I love you — I love you." What beautiful words, none more so... no... Must be thousands of times in each lifetime, and meaningless. The most important words that can be, the only gift worth giving, and completely without significance. I love you — I love you — I love you — I love you — hollow words from hollow people... This should suffice, no need to say more... Yet, it doesn't. Yes, I know. How well I know it should, how many things should. The world should. It doesn't... no. Will it ever? I will — I do — perhaps you will... listen — I don't want to talk to idiots. They don't read me anyway... But I

love you — I love you — I love you — I love you — I
reach out for the words — open to them... let them
in. Sweet music, sweet acceptance music, sweet you're
needed music, sweet together music... Stinking lie.
Diarrhea of the mouth. I love you... where's the I —
I love you... there is no I — I love you... where is
the I, where is the I, where is the I. How simple,
how sweet — I love you. To hell with you bitch, there
is no you, I swing at you with my mind, go right
through, no substance, hollow — one, altruist, empty
of self, selfless Self-less one. I don't hate you —
no, hollow one, I'm trying to fill you. I love you — I
love you — I love you — I love you — where's the I,
where's the — the raving, Wulf... Dissect I love you?
Yes, let's... It's beautiful at the beach today. I
love you — ditto — ditto — ditto — I love you — I open to
you — I feel you — I understand you — I believe you —
I need you — I give to you — ditto ditto — I am one
with you — all together, all these and more, many
more, say love. I love you, ditto, ditto. I roll over
on the blanket and write my name on the inside of
Alianne's thigh, up close, she laughs, wets her
finger, erases it. Her husband would frown on this.
She's wonderful when I'm working, never bothers me,
likes that I'm a writer — she's great. I love you...
Where's the I? Can you give me something you don't
have? You grant me love. Do you have it to give? Can
you give me something not possessed... you must be
love. You must be love to give love... are you love?
Hollow one, are you love? Point to yourself and say,
"I give you my love." If you give me your love, you
must have love to give. Consider the source. If the
giver is empty, hollow, I disregard the word. I love
you — I give you my love. You love? Are you love? Is
your love you? Do you love yourSelf? If you don't
love the Self, the I, then why should I? What
possible importance could I attach to what it says?
Should I give credence to a nonexistent thing? Love

can only come from love. A vacuum can fill nothing.
You can't give a thing you don't have. To attempt
this — chaos. Fill yourself with love, saturate
yourself, become the thing, then... "I love you,"
becomes a blessing... touched with life... full,
rich, bursting with it... Yes... I'm watching some
slob wobble across the clean, white Pacific sand —
what an offensive sight, degrading. I should follow
her into the water and hold her under till the
bubbles give up... Come dear one, stand there,
beautiful in mind and body, full of living and
giving, not hollow... touch yourself, run your
hands over your body and mind, caressing... fall in
love... you are worth love you know... start with
the good of you... hold it... love it... it spreads
fast... come, dear one, fall in love... Give, yes,
give what you have, and when you look around you'll
have more, give to her, give to him, give to yourself.
How can you gain by giving? I'm laughing it's so
simple, yes, really laughable. How can I gain by
giving? How can you grow by giving? There is no
other way. I really only live in your eyes, you live
only in mine. Don't you see, when you give to me of
yourself... my eyes thank you. I accept your gift.
If the gift was of you, I accept you... "bought"...
yes. Dear one, this is life. When I answer a word
or thought or gesture of you with a Yes... you come
alive, only then, with my Yes. You come alive...
Alone is wonderful, necessary... but without my Yes
to accompany you, waiting for you, it's the blackest
pit of eternity.

Are you sick of the word Love as I am? Let's
start a movement, a cult. You can be president and
you can be treasurer. Don't expect me to come to your
goddamned meetings, you multi-reflected idiots.

These sagging resigned paltry fractional truths
— my meager offering to this ball-less de-ovaried

world — where there is no sin, original or modified —
where each is weak and only the strong know of
theirs — where a guy roamed the streets of Paris
silently calling his loneliness; I think it was,
I'll admit, I know, it was me — where most songs of
hope are just cerebral cyclones — where the only
coherence is incoherent gibberish from a tortured
ragamuffin — hmmmmm yes — where most pregnancies
are the spawn of the incorrigibly stupid — where
the road to success is paved with nice guys — where
most everyone is a juice-sucking blotter — where
understanding equals isolation — where pure
emotions and tears of grief and joy are things of
shame — where cities entomb alive — where living in
notes and on paper and ink, slow death — where the
sound of laughing is a lonely sound — where a
uterus is only a whoopie-shoot — where the measure of
talent is the breadth of the audience — where the
Real of life is pornographic — where jazz and rock
are disdained because "culture" is based on antiquity
— and the new and feared are disdained — where not
the substance but the sign and shape of mimicry
is the IN password — where each dawning a glorious
new excitement, and still I don't want to leave
this fucked-up world.

     She said please, no, please don't close your
eyes — like that you could be making this love with
anyone, and I want to know you are with me — watch
me while I kiss you here and make you happy — when
I don't feel your eyes on me, I'm alone and ashamed;
and I did, and she beautiful warm-tongued and
lipped and voiced "O I love you, love you Wulf, I
love you."

     No I'm not truth, you imbecile. Yes! You've
called me this — a lie — much of this is a lie — can
you see it? When I lie? No! I'll never lie to you —

but part of me is a lie — inherent, congenital liar —
there's no answer for this — no way out... Accept
this thing here in me — in you — perceptivity
sensitivity awareness — we're lost without it...
Without it my lie becomes your truth, your truth-lie
becomes the truth-lie-lie of another, and the truth-
lie-lie-lie of others, and on, and on, and on, and on.

The only thing more ridiculous than the rich
are the poor. I'm tired, bored, half seasick; it's the
biggest liner in the world. Britain rules the seas.
The Queen Elizabeth, Third Class Tourist. I didn't
want to cross the Atlantic on a damned pleasure
boat — their pleasure has never been mine — I knew
this would be no exception. I wanted to escape all
this by taking a freighter but none were leaving,
so here I am. Really offensive is the effort they
make to emulate First Class. Trying to give the
passengers a taste of everything they'd have in a
more expensive passage, and the efforts are pathetic;
every night a little four-piece out-of-tune orchestra
plays for dancing, with all the usual trite business
about changing partners, ladies' choice, and all
that crud. These idiots eat it up. The room where
these tired rituals are performed: the "Winter
Garden" — Winter Garden! What the hell, it's like
any other third class beer hall. Let's face it, when
it comes to being banal, Britain still rules the
seas.

Traveling! Always thrown in with "the people" —
no escape, day after day, and everywhere you look,
these clowns. Idiots, trying to social it up. Pathetic
little girls dying for shipboard romance, and the
men all horny. No, I don't believe they're even horny,
they just feel they should be — it's a black-mark,
crossing to Europe on a liner and not getting laid.
So ball it up kiddies, you'll have your experiences
to talk about and those abominable pictures you're

incessantly taking. 'Course, you weren't having fun, but it sounds and looks like you were.

The cabins? I can't believe these accommodations — four people in a diminutive box, smelly ventilation (portholes are not for the tourist caste). Why four people in a cabin barely large enough for one? They know what they are doing, what the people want: playrooms, cocktail lounge, dance hall, theatre, on and on — there's no room left for larger cabins or privacy. The clowns aren't interested in privacy. Social sardines.

Her voice, its sensualled accent — her rich female-toned voice, turned me ever on. I hear it now... Yes, listen to the voices — go quiet, relax — listen to the voices — the hard flat ones — the precise, carefully articulated ones — the o so compelling, sex-modulated ones — the wind-up tin-sound-box ones — o yes, listen t-h-r-u the words — listen for lovelife or death-rattle — If you would live with Love: Think upon those warm vital breath-giving — remember now, can you, the life-pulse tones singing good. Listen to the voices. Think upon the love cannibals, flesh eaters — hear now, can you, the death-noise hiding.

Listen to the voices. Can you hear the lovelies? — Or has black wing flutter grim-din-deafed you... Ah, her voice...

I remember the Gare St. Lazare — all the way across the Atlantic and the train whistling through the picturebook French countryside from Cherbourg to Paris and my wanting of her kept building. I got off the train and no Alianne and I was sadly strangely empty standing as if alone there in the bustling depot and then I felt hesitant, tentative fingers on my cheek; I turned and there was her face and she came into my world so fast that as I think back — I remember, it felt like a soft wind blowing right through me, filling

me with her fragrance. We walked out into the city,
sat in a park... And autumn was scraping her
palette over Paris.

The way she could look at me — a look of
complete concentration — a thing of the moment —
complete in itself. She'd say, "No, don't look away —
stay — stay, let me look in your eyes" — and again,
each time again I would begin afraid; and yes, I
never could really look — now that I think on it, I
only once really looked. I know now that there, in
her exquisite eyes — no, through them... was Truth —
Truth — the deep bottomless truth sought by all
humankind. And little man that I am, I would look
away and bury my face in her hair, or in a pillow
stained with us. But he — her legal lover who waits —
he would never see it — will never see it; for I have
seen him and he doesn't know there is such a thing
to see in a pair of human eyes, that everything to
know can be known in that instant. No, he'll never
look, and I couldn't keep looking. But I know it is
there to see — like it is in a summer day or a storm
on the sea — or a gull on the wind — or a panther
stalking his prey — or the fire down deep in our
earth — or the immeasurable cold of space... And in
her eyes — o sweet Truth yes, in her eyes, all
spelled out for me, and I couldn't keep reading... I
never fucked her, or balled her, or laid her, or did
anything to her — No — we made love together —
together — together — I never ate her, or went down
on her, or did anything... to her — but together.
Yes, together — not to, but with. How many can you do
a thing with? Everybody wants to be laid; but how
many want to make love? So few. Do you? Are you
sure? Have you ever really shared anything in
life? Really shared it with another? Be Truthful.
I laugh at the theologians and their constant
prattle of truth — truth — truth. I've never talked
to one who even suspicioned that the Only Way To

Truth Is By Being Truthful. "Know the truth, and
the truth shall make you free." That poor sainted
bastard tried to tell them — and they nailed him up.
What is more terrifying to a shackled man than
freedom? The freedom to sail off the edge of a flat
world — or to fly a kite in an electrical storm — or
to say "Know the truth and the truth shall make
you free"... and the truth was in her eyes. Can you
believe it — believe that truth can be found in a
pair of human eyes? No? Where then? In a book — the
Bible — Hemingway — a sermon — a talk with God — a
pair of human eyes? I hope for your sake — and mine
— one day you see. I can't tell you where to look —
no, only the when and where of my failure.

I must have cried for hours, all the time we
were talking and even while we were loving.
Tomorrow she'd climb on that goddamned plane and
fly off to the dear old U.S.A., dear old Hollywood,
dear old Laurel Canyon, and her dear old husband.
To him, she had about as much depth as this paper
I'm writing on. She — so deeply female; when I loved
her, I felt I had in my arms all women all through
the ages, from her on back to whatever the beginning,
all the flesh, smiles, caresses, tenderness, violence,
joy, coming, all of these things and so many more —
so many more were her. Yes, to me she was all women,
and not an ounce of competitiveness in her whole
emotional being, no genital-jealousy game, never —
no, never a trace. When she smiled on you, you knew
you had been smiled on by woman, and if her eyes
were saying love or fright, then inside those are
the things that were happening, they were true
things, her eyes were. This may sound strange to
you if you have never experienced the thing I'm
writing about.

You've read or heard or suspected, and you

can "perhaps." You've seen or tasted or touched or
smelt or felt and you can "know." This is what I
know — in the little bistro I told her about Remarque
and his Arc de Triomphe and Ravic and we drank
Calvados and she sat next to me — each to ourselves,
close, though not touching; and with her making a
small sound I looked and her eyes swimming full of
love for me and when we kept looking and more and
more I felt as though I were inside her, though not
moving, and her eyes overflowed with wonder — "O
Wulf... I come... so much I love you!" And all so
very tender and such a lovely gift; and I know a
seldom, perhaps never-before thing. How lovefull of
woman — she... my Alianne. Perhaps the greatest
confession of my youthful cowardice — I never looked
again — not like that.

Ah, no wonder she married short; perhaps
she's the only woman in our world, and perhaps
there isn't a man, and perhaps with a feeling way
down she suspected this. To give a world and get
small change — no, perhaps not one who believed in
the True worth of his life, his love, his cock. If I
would ever bless you, it would be to bless into your
life such holy-wholly completeness in your mate,
dear ones. This I know now — in her so very rare,
unashamed womanhood, the womb of the man world —
after loving such a one, the games of sex leave you
yawning or crying-early-morning-after long walks.

How I loved that woman. O that first day we
owned the City. She pointing, then laughing at my
little-boy delight, skipping and singing, walking
backwards to keep each new strangeness a little
longer, and our laughing — "No, it's not the pissoir
that breaks me up but the guys after, going on off
up the street nonchalantly buttoning their pants —
beautiful." She leading me through Metro tunnels
and cabs and cockeyed leaning little streets,
strange new-smell restaurants and snails — "No,

Wulf, you use this little thing to get them from
the shell, then, emmmmm, good" — and yes, and merry-
go-round spinning our quick Paris time, fast montage-
blurred into one abstract color-swirled memory, with
my eyes, and my ears, and my arms, all too small to
hold it, or her. And she was gone and I stayed sick
in my room and wrote out my pain... This.

And one night a dream came and told me I got
to her too late — she had sold herSelf into marital
bondage and a death had already maggoted the
flesh and lip to lip sucked the life and decay
thickened the air and I backed slowly and she last
gasped "Wulf, man must form the woman, yes you must
fashion her." And the heaven-made lovefull grayfull
eyes went opaque marbles and a death's head
fluoroscoped the lovefull face — and a millions-old
sob ranted rocketed through myself — and it haunts
me yet — while I cautious step through blood-wet
fields of dying whispering with quick quiet hope to
this and that one — How big is the death in you?

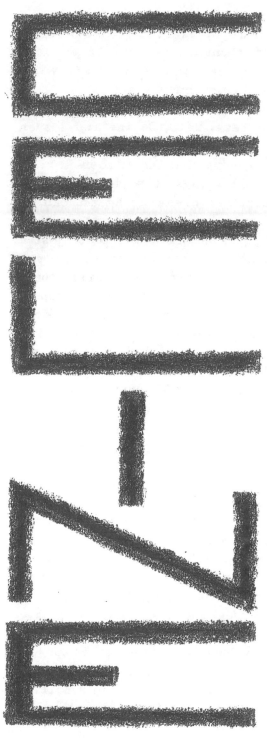

Then Celine
knocked at my
door... "Crazy
American! Sure you
be sick, always in
the room." Off we
go to see her
Paris; and it's
like we're going to
run the wheels
off that little
Renault she drives.
We're very touristy,
criss-crossing the
city; even a Sunday
at Versailles —
kids us, chasing
each other through
the hallowed
King-walked
gardens, hide-go-
seek in the Bois.
The Tour Eiffel
clear to the top
and she kind of
acrophobic but
alright after a
bit, and while up
there meeting a
"Sorbonne" American
who wants me to
hitchhike to
Spain with him,
and Celine — cute,
holding my arm —
"he stay in Paris"
meaning it. John
Garode's his name:

nice guy, perennial student — we liked each other —
who later introduced me to "Pierre": good-deal black-
market money-changer (though John himself got later
taken to the melody of one hundred and thirty
dollars on an Arab-sharpie money swap).

Most places she'd never been: blasé Parisians,
New Yorkers — all the same. Hell, Celine and I even
took the boat trip River Seineing through the city;
and so bitching cold, we're shaking harder from
laughing than cold and always, any time after, she
or I saying "boat trip" we break up again 'cause
that's the coldest bit I've ever been in; it really
wasn't too smart, with my not having a coat, just a
light California jacket... and next day in the rain
we walk for hours trying to find me a duffel coat I
could afford and a pair of those fur-lined European-
style winter shoes. And by the time we get back to
Rue de Courcelles, she's so wrung out with dancing
all night and leading me around interpreting and
showing and shopping, she can hardly make it to
the club. But what a big-hearted, easy-giving girl,
always bringing me crazy little French pastries
and such; and even when I kept going to the same
Blvd. St. Michel shop window digging a pair of
Italian-cut pants real popular in Paris... next
thing — "I want you to have them" — too much!

And pretty quick I'm out of money, talking of
boating back to U.S. and she — "No better you stay
with me." Now look, she was frightened; saying this
was no easy thing, she and I both knew she was
vulnerable as hell; a few years earlier she'd been
through a marriage with a psycho painter, she loved
him and it had been rough, and since then she'd
kind of reclused it. When I met her, she's Can-Can
dancing at the Moulin Rouge and practically nothing
social; she'd tried the lesbian whirl but nothing or
nobody moved her so she kind of built up a little
world of routine with her job and apartment and

her two cats: "Mimi" and "Osiris," her records and
books — "I know, I know," but at least she's making
it; it's got nothing to do with life but she would
never be able to sleeping-pill or river it... so you
can see "come live with me" was an uneasy thing for
her to say — but she did. Good to me! That girl was
good to me.

Sometimes I'd take her to work and use the
car; sometimes go to a show, or prowl Pigalle
dialoguing with the whores or the cool American
colored cats that swing so high in Paris pimping
French hustlers. But mostly I'd just hop the Metro
to St. Germain des Pres and maybe walk over to
Rue Valerne and see genius painter Ernst Fuchs —
who joined the church, became a saint to solve his
rampant libido problem and now free... tenderly
brush to canvas — and I'd sit digging his Dali-like
technique when and if there was enough light
through the one window, million-staired up to
studio. Or just-getting-famous-Howl-poet Allen
Ginsberg and his pummeled generation of Beat
angels. Or the end and epitome of weird-dom: Vali,
fantastic artist but the magazines only want to
print about her outrageous costumes and make-up and
dancing. Or confused befuddled Tony: married to
Boots, his hip show-business mother, who's actually
stand-up comic Lenny Bruce's mother and Tony always
laughing 'bout being Lenny's father-in-law and how
he's getting horny for the tender young — hungry-
eyeing through the strange city but Oedipus hooked.
Or Lee Forrest in her tranquil junk-shrouded grey
world — "Wulf, can you score for me tonight? I don't
think I can make it." Or Hans and Udo just back
from Moscow on some kind of artist exchange or
something and funny-fooling with the heavy Russian
authoritarianism — and bang! suddenly it's not
funny, and frightened a bit "Good to be back in
Paris." Or Gregory Corso: the only real angel poet

I've met; gone out of his mind but getting published
some, and so sweet and candid you've got to love him
with his sorry little plan to hide out in New York
with some menial job and nights walking—talking
up long lone poems. Or Allen's Peter: cool-sweet so
not sweet and lost-blind before and after Allen. Or
tired, love hungry five-language Georgette and her
brutal Teutonic ex-stormtrooper, who wants to iron-
glove marry her; and she "I'll translate you to the
French, Wulf" almost pure idiom into French?—Wow!
Or great-souled Raymond Ferra: Austrian-German
paratrooper. How did he live through it, the whole
war, all those years, jumping and cutting, slashing,
machine-gunning, and now poor beyond belief...
defeated little room in the old no-heat no-water
Hotel Alsace-Lorraine; winter-stiff fingers, drawing
in gloves or in bed when like usually there weren't
even enough francs for a little kerosene to burn in
an empty potage can on the floor; and always the
way his eyes showed happy when I came to his door;
and very much an artist and very uncommercial,
and "Do you have a cigarette?" Well shit, Europeans
are different—greater different—I guess. And
these are my kind of people: expendable to the world
till they come up with something too beautiful to
ignore. And with all their close-to-the-edge survival
they're living bigger than my waterskiing, picture-
producing, T-Bird-wheeling, starlet-laying, conning,
big wheeldeal friends back in ol' Hollywoodland.

Borrowing Celine's car reminds me of a time
I got so ridiculous high... Christmas Eve—and I
went to a party in a little Rive Gauche bookshop
directly across the Seine from Notre Dame: called
"Shakespeare & Co."—the proprietor: a renowned
literary friend of Gregory and Allen. And there—
sitting lovely Lee now ever lost to me, stoned out,
junked out, as all there. And it being midnight:
Peter, Allen, me, and a young poet whose name I

could see I should have known but didn't, cross
the bridge to Christmas Midnight-Mass Notre Dame...
How strange! Thousands of people, you could hardly
move and not a sound, then the great cathedral
organ weaving a thin melodic pattern way high-up
the scale and every so often here and there hooded
monks with little bells, ting ting... ting ting...
ting ting, and it's all lit by hundreds of these
flickering candles — awesome beautiful — not religious
but eerie beautiful — scene I'll never forget.

And when coming back to the party I blast a
pipe-full of Gregory's hashish, and like in nothing
flat I'm so far out of it and frightened: cause at
2:15 I'm supposed to be wheeling up in front of
Moulin Rouge for Celine — who's been sickish lately —
show must go on and all — and here I can't even
scratch my head without wondering what my hand is
doing up there. Drive across Paris Christmas Eve!
Man "straight" I can't get across that town without
coming-up lost. Can't let her down, standing sick
from me out in the cold, all danced out and loving
me and I don't show — no, it's not going to be like
that; I've got an hour and a half to make it and
it's a twenty minute drive... but for me to even
drive, much less orient myself in this traffic!

Next thing, there I'm sitting in the Renault —
how? I don't know — motor running and oh so careful
unpark it "easy" two blocks, turn right, Blvd. St.
Germain, left and so forth — can't miss; next thing
I'm blinking at a Dead-End street sign, nosed right
up to it, engine idling patiently — no watch, how
long been there... scared, a real scare-high, heart
beating like demented, and picking up that sick
girl looms as the biggest thing in life to my soaring
hashish brain — and backing out, deep frightened.
A nightmare of wrong-way one-way streets, irate
gendarmes, profane French cab-drivers, more dead-
ends, lost — lost — lost and, miraculously, plink,

plank plunk, cooly tires gently swishing the curb
in front of famous Moulin Rouge — two-fifteen and
she, just coming out and I'm saying, "Hi honey, say
you mind driving home?"

Lots of nights I'd just stay in writing,
usually in bed to keep warm and save the gas, and
at about two-thirty the cats would go to the window,
sitting on the sill, eyeing the street, making
little impatient cat sounds — soon as they heard the
Renault, quick to the door... key rattling in lock
comes Celine, big-warm-grinned, happy-faced to see
me and she'd make hot tea and toast for us in bed;
then she'd turn to me with that constant unbartering
love of hers gushing good. Yes, it was a good time
for her and me too.

Seeing Celine in pictures on all the walls:
modeling hats, suits, dresses, so assured, self-
assured and inside all the time the buzz-saw, meat-
saw chewing away; shots of her: modern ballet, Can-
Can, happy smile and inside hamburger.

But then there were nights when she'd hurry
home and eager-bust into the place and here I'd be
foraging over maps and sailing times: North Africa,
Palma, Majorca, Sicily — California boy wants back
to the sun, and it killed her, but man she never
bitched, just kept giving, even helping me translate
the French travel folders... and then of course she
starts missing periods and gets very frightened.

And all her dreams were drowned in tears.
Celine is pregnant. What a lovely thing, pregnant
with my child and so afraid. She said perhaps it
would be a boy and we laughed — a little Wulf, a
little bearded-one, silly fun — not for long. She is
frightened, really frightened. No, not of the child
nor of me — of the city: cold friendless city, city of
fear, she loved. Aren't they all?

She already knew two marriages had finished
me with that bit, but I really wanted the kid,

"Celine the baby is the important thing, you're thirty-three, this might be your last time!" I logic and philosophy all over the place: like as problems came up they wouldn't be problems but just more living "To hell with the future! We'll live it when we get to it" and "Who knows? Look I might sell big, famous and all, money enough for everything" and I'd go home and sell my house and the "Triumph"— we'd make it.

She is thirty-three, Celine is, she loves me, Celine does, and afraid to have a child; it would change her life — she hates her life: it is a thing to hate — really. Perhaps she is right; who am I to tamper with a lost soul's fences? Those fences work — don't they! Yes, San Quentin and Devil's Island and Bedlam work — don't they! Yes, who am I to destroy working functional things?

Now what she really needed then was a guy who thought conventional, but then she wouldn't love him — so nothing. I tried to show her how a child would fresh-life her, that that's what was great about children; but the city had consumed too much of her naturalness and what she felt was trapped — not holy. And rightly or weakly, I don't know which, I helped her plan the death of a life that was half mine... the-to-be-raised-in-the-old-world-child, I wanted so much.

Tomorrow is Christmas — thank God they called only one your son: we couldn't stand it twice a year. Celine doesn't want the child "yes, yes" but she is frightened — poor frightened thing. And the Police: how incongruous! The police are watching us — is the liberal French philosophy a lie... it's her womb, her blood she sheds, her fear, her death; keep your stinking hands from her. How small my voice sounds to me now. What have police to do with blood and murders planned on Christmas Eve?

I don't want to hurt you — but I do — I don't

want to pain you but I do — I don't want to run
from you but I do — I don't want to force your tears
— but I do — I don't want to pursue you — but I do — I
don't want to laugh at you — but I do — I don't want
to sex with you but I do — I don't want to genuflect
to you — but I do — I don't want to touch you — but I
do — I don't want to murder you — but I do — I don't
want to hate you — but I do — I don't want to taste
you — but I do — I don't want to love you — but I do.

　　If I were ever to fall in love with a people,
that would be the time I'd do it... Celine in her
hospital room and every day boys and girls from the
show, and mother, father, brothers, sisters, second
third fourth cousins, the place crawling with
Frenchmen and so child-like delighted with cranking
her bed up and down, eating her candy, jokes, good-
cheering her; mother and sister "fantastic" day-and-
night gently caring her. No one speaks English; I
sit bedside holding her sick hand; her father right
across the bed; I'm her lover knocked their daughter,
sister, friend up; broke, no money to help and now
I'm leaving in a day or two for America — the whole
thing's costing the family many thousands — with an
infected ovary and fallopian tube simultaneously
carved out, much against my diet-therapy type protests.
Not only was there no American-like shotgun introduced
onto the scene, not once did papa sitting across the
bed even dirty-look me, nor mama, nor sister... man
they cried when I left, cried for Celine and her
pain and mine, and the futility they felt in their
own lives and in ours — they loved me.

　　I'm going back someday soon to the human
side of the Atlantic.

　　That beautiful story of the South Seas, where
a child is a child, where there are no bastards —
true — yes — a child is a child. No — not in America,

or Europe, but there, yes. Yes there is much that is true there. Gauguin — didn't he find love there? Maugham said so — I can believe this; there could be love in such a place... Perhaps there Celine could open the heart of her soul to a child and let it speak — lips to breast — fulfillment — birthright (yes, very!). Yes, they could love a child, where a child is a child, a mother is a mother, a name is a name: a thing to call you by, an aid: not a necessity nor a ridiculous symbol of acceptance "a rose by any other" a child is a child. They tell me that there, there in the sun islands — how precious are the children: each family, any family would take it, feed it, love it... Who was the father? Who was the mother? What is his blood? Is he black or white or green or blue? Who could care? It's a child, a thing to love, a thing to love you — a gigantic thought — a thing to love you, a thing that will love you. No — not in the city. Yes — on the island. Yes, the land and the sky are benevolent, not brutal. New York, Paris, Los Angeles — cities stinking with struggle, stinking with sophistry, oozing with corruption. Each must eat the other. Yes — I understand the ancient laws. Yes — the jungle laws. Yes — we are animals, but gods too... Too wondrous for cannibalism. But then, yes I know... this is the frightening thing... to be a god can terrify. I know: Karl Marx told me so — poor frightened little man, with his adding machine for a soul — where humans are digits on a long white paper scroll off into infinity. And now one half of the world pushed itself onto his monstrous image. Mouse-man, born too soon — the age of automaton was made for him... So sad! Yes! Very!

If I could reach inside her and pull myself out I think I would do it, like an abortion, corruptment, clean out the womb of her love, empty of me. The pathos in her eyes wrenches me, twists itself inside me. How long must the pain of me, the hate of me, the need of me, how long must it lie there inside her festering, live there inside, hurting her... I don't want her hurting. Sweet tender thing, sweet lost thing she is. Cutting me, chopping me, berating me — the names — then barely audible, quietly in the middle of it all, "You could stay with me, you know — I need you now" and eyes like a lost little animal: lost in the city of tombs that became a tomb; where each night she goes to dance her inane dance. Dance of fools, for fools and she knows. O yes! Really knows, really understands how foolish her dance, her life. Not a good thing, her understanding — no a bad thing her understanding: killing her, the understanding is; knows it's a maze, knowing of a maze, knowing no way out. House of mirrors life... someone got her in. "God is in heaven — can't someone get me out?" she cries mutely to me through a smile she fixed.

I couldn't leave, just couldn't leave that hospital room... How can I write this now? It was only minutes ago I stood there "Write me as soon you get to New York, darling — I will like to know how you have make the trip" all in that crazy French-hashed English I love so much. My god, the monster I am, I know it now — she lies there, her belly full of my child — gorged with pain and me splashing tears over her sweet neck... come to say my goodbyes, and she "Please go darling I can stand no more, you must leave" and she's crying and I'm just tearing her up more and I can't — I keep trying — can't make the door, can't let her fingers pull from mine; lying there so pale — I consumed her — she knows it — I know it — she loves me... Any time, any time, right down the line — just one "All right honey — together. Let's do it like that — together" and I'm loved, I'm a father again. Chicken-shit coward, what am I waiting for — a saint who's great sex? Grow up Wulf! You who's had so much love — oh I don't know! It's so close, just minutes back... so pale, so sweet, so forgiving, so loving and tough. Good lord, how tough that girl: I gave it to her — really, and flat on her back, too weak to fight, and eyes full of tears and love "Darling, you must go, I can stand no more — really — I want you kill me: to stop all this — let's die — do it to us or go — honey, please."

Then just all of a sudden I did it: turned my back on her and went slowly through the door — it was like sleepwalking — I started closing the door and it wouldn't go — you know, the closing door and the symbolisms and all, but then I did it... Just pushed it closed and it clicked shut, and it was the most final sounding sound I've ever heard. Oh just to pull the damn thing open and say "together" — Couldn't see a thing all the way down those hospital stairs and down the rainy street where I stopped at her sister's charcuterie shop to get the cat feed — I tried not to look at her because I knew — she looked at my face and started crying — and me too. She shoved a couple of jambon sandwiches in my coat pocket with "Bon voyage, Wulf" and I barely made it to the door before I came apart and it was like that clear to the apartment with people staring like they will.

Really can two human beings feel such a gigantic need for each other — need to hold and protect each other, help the other through the vicious ruthlessness of this fucked-up world and then part? One can — I did. Insipid tragic fool that I am. CAN'T WRITE ANYMORE — IT'S TWISTING THE KNIFE — "HELL WITH IT!"

I fed the cats, picked up my bags, both cats watching me, one long last look at the apartment — our apartment, a dry sob comes from nowhere, I'm frightened, little boy lost... I didn't think I could do it but I did — slammed the door — it locked —

the key inside on the table — that's it — it's done.

O the place looked empty on that last look: the gay ballet poster, her dancing and modeling pictures, watercolors from friends, my dirty dishes... How unbelievably lonely it looked — empty of us. She had to come back to that, back to little bits of me stuck everywhere: me in an old subway ticket, and used razor blades, dirty sheets, notes to her of old and hers to me. Ghosts are hard to clean out, and come upon suddenly — the spectre of lost-love in one forlorn forgotten sock can suck the wind out of you — I know, yes I know... so why, why why — I don't know, I don't know, I only know it hurts — it's so new and hurts so much.

How did I get to the train? Really, how? Through the faithful old rackety Metro, with Saturday night fun-watchers reveling and here and there one sober face wondering about my hurting. Then out of the tunnels, walking and resting every so little to the depot with my selfsame heavy defeated luggage... and all the time one large gob of pain — getting too old for the Don Juan bit... this one got me — yes with eyes full of candor and the sweet, simple, direct "I love you" — How could I do it? What do we humans think we are? There is just so much pain an animal can bear!

Look at them out there: happy smiling faces, smiling happy bon voyages. Gare du Nord Station — "Au revoir Paris — au revoir." My stomach in knots; I'm hurting "Celine — Celine — Celine — au revoir Celine." And that screechy tin-whistle European train call and the clickity clicking wheels — all a counterpoint obligato to the guilt and waste and pain of my sad useless goodbye... click-click, click-click, click-click. Tomorrow I'll walk through London. Tonight I'm heavy, so very heavy with emptiness — empty of love-hope, empty of Celine — click-click, click-click — au revoir Celine — click-

click — au revoir Paris — click-click — can it be, is
it? And Why? Great whys — where am I going? And
I went — WHERE. . .? Where can a train take you?
Why am I going? To whom? To what? I, and the
dreary drizzling Paris streets wept our perhaps
never again goodbye.

Vali Myers — I heard so much of her from kids in Hollywood who had made the Paris scene—she was kind of like the queen of the existentialists when that funny Sartre thing was happening and she, like most of the kids that gave the movement its color/flavor, didn't know Sartre from Gide. And why should they, frantic-balling everything in sight: summer, sleeping under the bridges; winter, on the Metro gates. Scrounging for a little night-warmth. To eat, stay high: selling anything they had, a pencil-sketch, a piece of carved wood, a poem, themselves — and Vali of the wild little thin face and body, hysteria nymphing up and down the sex side of the Seine — notorious Vali, most of her real life in Paris and never bothered to speak French, and why — nights when she danced her penis-pulsing Afro-Vali rhythm at Bal Afrique, that was all the talking necessary for her needs.

A night at the old old Hotel Alsace-Lorraine and Vali's showing me her weirdly lovely diminutive drawings and about books and what my writing meant to me and about the Dutch photographer Van Der Elsken who compiled that book on her *Love on the Left Bank*, the best thing I've seen on the Left Bank frenzied ones — and in comes this guy Tony, kind of unhip USA-ish and he fellow-

Americans me all over the place — he's a hair
stylist, works for Gene Jacovie, young successful
Beverly Hills type I knew from the States, so I
go along some.

Funny how things move — few days later Tony
calls, says he's dying to talk to an American. So,
though it was a drag, I meet him and he wants to
go score. "We can walk. It's on the Rue Bonaparte
right down from 'Café Bonaparte.' Man, this chick
is the strangest, like she's a junkie and she stays
high all winter writing poetry and only comes down
in the spring, but she always has a few joints
around." OK! — and that's my first time in the Hotel
de Londres and the first time I know of Lee.

I said, "Stop licking your chops" and that's the
way it was you know, licking them in anticipation.
She hadn't had a fix in too long and all the time
we're lying on the bed with the blankets over us to
keep out that god damned Paris winter, she kept
twitching, running her hands over her arms and
body, like trying to brush away something. She
said she was glad I was there, she couldn't score
till twelve-thirty and the time wasn't moving. So
we talked, filled it up that way. You know, I don't
think too much one way or the other about the
hipsters that are hung-up on junk, but this pretty
little girl, rotting to hell in that tired old room,
with no money, no friends except a few starving
poets and artists, most of whom as wrung out and
famine-poor as she — and here she's trying to feed a
habit. Well, she hadn't really intended to kick till
spring, the gnawing French winter frightened her
so; but with being behind in the rent, nothing for
food, and a three-thousand-franc each and every
week habit around her neck, she'd tried to kick
it. But that old world is just too cold and lonely
sometimes without a friend, and the stuff was as
good and faithful — no, better and more faithful

than any she'd had till then, but like so many you
call friend, when you try to put them down, they can
get mean, real mean. And her friend had gotten
mean.

So there we were on a shivery December
morning, pushing our way through the ridiculous
cold, vainly trying to hurry, with that little
puppy of hers pulling on his leash, stopping every
few feet to piss or shit or inspect some other pup's
work, but even with being so eager and her body
crying like it was, she smiled that hurt sweet
smile and coaxed him in her child-voiced, little-
girl French. She loved that little dog. I left her
in front of a café on the Blvd. St. Germain — left
her to score, and walking to the Metro with her "See
you tomorrow" I got thinking about her room, where
every scrap of paper holds a poem or two, and how
some of them so soft and tender told me of her
softness and her tenderness, and what more can you
ask of a poem? I thought about her in Hollywood —
that tough town, and how it must have stomped her
with its rough-shod fame-money avariciousness,
ground the poet and her dear, little, scribbled bits of
self into its dirt. Hollywood: so hard and shiny and
bright and pitiless, and the carnivorous dykes and johns
and playgirls, clawing and plucking and fucking and
sucking her down — down into the soft white pus, the
soft decay there under the glib, tinsel, tinkling
laughter. And everyone all mirrored, reflected in
the polished lacquered success wagons, fish-tail
Caddy and T-Birds and the funny who-do-you-know —
I-know-him-her Name-Game everywhere, the Strip,
Frascati's, Schwab's, and even in the Canyon, if-
you're-anyone-you-know-someone mirror. And she the
girl saw only the reflections and played the town's
game. And she the poet could see — yes, could see
through the mirror and through the games... and
the schizo.

So the poet was dying and came to Paris,
where they'll let you rot if you will. And of course
there, left of the Seine, alone with her old friend,
and her pen, and her dreams, she did... did rot.
And sometimes the city, the great patron city, blew
on the spark that glowed there deep inside. The
spark that was her poet's heart. And sometimes it
became bright for awhile and cooled and there in
the ashes... sometimes a poem.

The Beast was smiling — and blood on his
teeth.

Then all-girl girl-Lee, liking my writing and
very-much me, says she wants me to meet a close-
favored friend — Allen Ginsberg, much high-sung
North Beach poet, called "beat" then — well, why not?
And so we walked along the Seine and she tells me
of pretty Peter, Allen's never-separated-from world
traveler boy. Twenty-six Cit le Coeur it was I think
and nobody's home, so we anyway hang awhile and
fish some potatoes and a little meat from what
turned out to be real good stew — nobody had money
but always some kind of eclectic stew on the stove;
I really believe it was the same one, you know, a
big pot and adding different goodies all the time,
like a perennial goulash or whatever. We hung
around awhile after we ate but I had to catch my
Metro train before one o'clock; I walked Lee back to
Rue Bonaparte and ran for the station, and must
have been about half a block away when she called
"Wulf, if you miss that last train you can stay with
me." I didn't, but did some nights later and it was
very strange. I hadn't wanted to lay her because
of Celine and all the rest of it, but I really dug
talking to her, and even with the broken front
tooth, looking was getting nicer all the time.
Anyway, it was some time later before I stayed and
by then we're both pretty well hung, but for the

same reasons I didn't want a sex thing, which made
for one of the strangest and in a way lovely nights
I'd ever spent with a girl.

I'd missed the last train again and just too
tired to walk all the way across Paris and it was
raining too. How strange in bed, here I'm loaded with
compassion and lots of tenderness feelings for her
lost-girl scene, and it's really very obvious she wants
me in a good way, nice way. I feel the length of her
nudeness along me and with her poet's mind and hands
she touches me in a kind of haunting, getting-to-know-
me, hands and fingers gently searching and pressing
softly so very endearingly over my skin way — and I
too, imitatively. How strange — all night I don't think
we slept much, just did this, I can still feel her
fingers cupping my shoulder cap and that never-will-
forget reptile-like smooth/rough skin of hers. Imagine
practically a whole night like that, a good, glad-
that-I-had-night, and then after when living together
we sexed not too often, but the same close together
unity of give and take we'd found that first night.

I got her to go to the free-if-you're-broke
American Hospital they used to have in Paris — I
guess maybe they did this to keep the expatriate
Americans from getting to look too seedy and thereby
reflecting on mother country. Well anyway, with the
hole in her sweet smile filled, girls just didn't
come any more girlsome. Then we started with kicking
the junk, and of course that was the end.

We were always talking of the sun; Mexico,
North Africa, idyllic hand-in-hand word pictures on
sunwashed beaches with big neverending blue domed
over us; god, it was cold that winter, and I don't
want to talk about the catastrophic time when I took
away her candy — not right now anyway.

Jean Fransoir, picture-taker, writer for the
French mag *Jour de France*. Wanting to write deeper
stuff, but a dingy feeling of minute self-worth

drying out his pen. Really very nice guy — Lee's old love — me being her new — and true to his big heart wanting us together if it was a true good thing between us. I remember the night we found her sitting in the Deux Magots — we stopped to watch her, unnoticed. I said "Who wouldn't love her." He glanced towards me and smiled. True, who wouldn't love her, all the sweetness of childhood, the passion and warmth of womanhood, and the fucking junk.

All the Lucifers have angelic faces.

The form of her body; a Renaissance painter's dream; strange to modern me, but womanly, so of course wonderful. The feel of her dehydrated junkie skin, body; like making love to a dry lizard, or perhaps a rougher-than-usual snake — really, the strangest feeling skin you can imagine! All over her the same — the same tantalizing roughness, and yet soft, so incredibly soft and girl — but still, like some kind of snake under my hands. A smoother one: not really wild-river-snake — like that too — smooth like that; and it moved me quite a bit. Different, you know. Lots are silky, which is good — but a snaky skin — Yes! The musk of her — that could really rile me up, the musk from her crotch — aphrodisiac — the end! The clean-cut American would say she stank. Perhaps, but in Paris we all did... And I couldn't see her hanging out with a crew-cut anyway. In Paris she reeked, she polluted the air, stank — Yes... stank of yestersex... And what more can a woman do? We had a towel; we'd rub ourselves, drying ourselves with it after. She said "Don't use it on your face — I use it here." I said "Are you kidding?" and day after day it kept getting better, riper. It got so, we'd get high on that damn towel — I couldn't dry my face but we'd be in bed; you know, it was like putting my face right up inside her, and I would. We got hooked on that towel — till the maid found it one day — and washed it.

Nature boy and the junkie — too improbable to last. Her 15-minute-later denials of what was said or done, her love for the pose, the elegant, the phantasy, the back door out, and her shadow-grey world told me, tapped at the back of my consciousness. How could I listen, stop building dream castles in the sun for her, with her incredible fullness in bed, her wild uncalculated yet relaxed abandon, those inspiring encouraging endearing little cries and yelps of fulfillment and acceptance, all that, and the eternal sweetness. We kidded about the sounds, how they must have made the night girl on the switchboard horny as hell. No sound insulation in the Hotel de Londres. There really didn't need to be; the French expect you to make love. Lee said, "I hadn't had a man in here in so long, the concierge was worried for me." It must have been like that — the next afternoon, on our way out, she beamed, with her "Bonsoir Monsieur, bonsoir Mademoiselle Lee." And how great, walking along the banks with her, watching the barges up and down river... touching. I really can't blame myself sometimes for going blind in love; such a good, good, good feeling. O how much I want it in my life — every day, and lasting. Yes, but sometimes I get frightened, close my eyes, and take what's offered. Sex without love is such a dry thing.

You know, Lee! I'm still in love with the memory of our little time.

And then after awhile she let her tongue slip in my ear gently and caressed and rolled my balls in her fingers gently. And I lying soft and warm and resting all inside her, answer her blood call and with each new pulse grow a little. And then I'm big and she full with me began to squeeze

around me. And relaxing and squeezing we lie so
still hardly breathing. Bodies touching here and
there. Squeezing coaxing and I felt her tremble
begin and I too. And our all and everything there
in a womb world. My trembling became a throb and I
began to spurt hot and deep she too. We tremulous
together as young branches in a high wind spoke
each other's name as if in prayer. Yes. Lie still
floating off in our aftersweetness. And then after
awhile she let her tongue slip in my ear gently.

To her, poet's words were solid tangible things,
real things of substance, of solidity, of worth, of
finality — no, not tools, but of themselves true. To
me: not true — to her: true. True to her and not to
me, but what have my believing and her believing to
do with truth — she drops a cup, it falls and breaks;
it falls because it must — my or her beliefs upon the
actions and reactions of this cup change nothing —
the cup must, we must — laws... yes — destiny, fate...
shit. Laws inexorable for you and I, and the cup,
and for Lee too, yes, for all of us. Yes, the essence,
the thing of myself... simplicity. Complexities —
complicated people believe the way out of a confusing
complexity — through more devious complexity. O wow!
Lee reads the above — "Darling you write powerful
things, but this — any schoolboy knows this, it's
nothing, such a simple thing." O Lee, beautiful Lee,
you love the simple people, love my simplicity — fear
my simplicity, fear my disdain of complex complexities,
my ridiculously simple solutions to world problems,
and ours, mine and yours, his and hers, simple
falling-cup philosophy.

And nights sleeping with the unending softness
of her breasts freeforming around my back — and
times one still half-curious, half-firm earth-brown
tip nuzzling in my armpit — and her palmful oh so
female formed, deep as life navelled belly, with
each dream-depth-breath gently presses and makes

love, undulating love to my spine — and two-body-
warmth-moistened skins clinging — and each slow
sleep breath caress, again and again, body
whispering — your woman, your woman, your woman...
and you talk of an after-heaven.

And Lee saying "All this stuff you read that
they keep pushing at you, the Art of Love and all
such trash, make the woman ready, spend time
preparing her — I like it, the forcing sometimes...
sometimes to be raped." Yes...

Me: What can you do when your insides are on
fire?
She: Cry.
Me: Sometimes you can't.
She: Kill yourself.
Me: Sometimes that's impossible; you're too wise
— or stupid.
She: Forget it.
Me: What if you can't forget; what if it keeps
chewing on your insides?
She: Chewing — I thought you said fire?
Me: It's not important; chewing or burning,
when it gets bad enough you flip.
She: Flip — how flip?
Me: When it's more than you can handle
emotionally; a momentary psychosis — you know,
crazed for a little while... you flip, like
screaming or hiding or just closing up — everyone's
different.
She: Yes.
Me: Yes shit! Don't "yes" me; don't be cool
with me. Looking at you, I know you've had it; the
cautious way you move and talk like you're walking
the edge of a pit — real careful.
She: Oh, man, you're too much.
Me: OK, forget it.

She: No. Look, if you've got something to say, say it but forget the mystery crap.

Me: Know something? I'll always be an enigma to someone who reads Rimbaud — you dig clowns.

She: He was no clown — he was beautiful.

Me: Beautiful? Sure "word" beautiful, but just another fucked-up faggot poet who knew nothing, believed in nothing except death — became a gun-runner or something just as ridiculous.

She: God, I've had it with you! You're really simple — you understand nothing. He was a beautiful boy; of course he was lost, but he was fine and sensitive.

Me: A morbid stupid imbecile. I'm sick of you and everyone like you. Christ you think you have problems; everyone I meet who shows anything, anything at all — who's intelligent enough to see how messed-up it all is... terrified — trying to smother the life from himself.

She: Look at you — look who's talking. Trying to ball every girl in Paris. "Is a fwightened iddle boy lookin f'is mommy?" Get out of my sight; I may regurgitate.

Me: You're goddamned right I'm frightened — I know about loneliness in a way that you never will. I don't go around joining your little escapist groups.

She: "Escapist groups" — what a corny line, and you're supposed to be a writer. Don't tell me I belong to a group.

Me: The hell you don't — nice, neat, well-defined; the heroin hide-outs.

She: What else can you expect? I'm sick and tired of the rudeness and cruelty, everyone's into it — every time I go out, there it is. What do you want of me? Christ, I can't take anymore. I've had it up to here, up to here, do you understand.

Me: Sure I understand. I see it too. I feel it too. But dulling the way you do dulls everything,

dulls every possibility of escape. Like this, you're
going to keep getting it until the day you check
yourself out. Like this I see no hope for you.

She: You mean, vicious son-of-a-bitch; you self-
righteous bastard — look at you standing there — if
you know of a way, tell me about it, why don't you...
if you know.

Me: I have.

She: O no not again! I give up! That's all!

Me: Too simple for you?

She: Childish.

Me: Thank you.

She: There you go again.

Me: Of course it's childish; of course it's
simple; of course it's elementary. You think the way
out of confusion is through more confusion... sorry.

She: "Leave Paris, find the sun, get rid of
the needle, get some exercise, eat right, put down
idiots" — your needle's stuck. Damn you — someone
tells you they've lost all their money, their wife
left them, haven't had a gig in two months, they're
ready to open a vein — and you come up with
something like, "Do you like to do push-ups?" Really
you're too far-out — really.

Me: Look girl, if a thing is profound, it's
simple. Real things are always elementary. Real people
are simple people. Real ideas are uncomplicated...

She: Okay. But telling a guy he's overcooking
his vegetables when he tells you his lip is gone; he
can't blow his horn anymore — oh wow!

Me: I can't help it, it's true. How can he
expect to keep saying beautiful things when his
insides are all shit; when his lungs are coated
with nicotine slime — his brain hasn't had a decent
meal in years? Fuck him; I say what I feel. Man it
takes real physical and mental stamina to keep
blowing the way he did.

She: What did he say after you talked to him?

Me: He started to cry.

She: I don't know about you! What did you say
to him really?

Me: I know what you mean. Sometimes I break
up when I'm talking to someone; I get a perspective
on how ludicrous the scene is and I've got to laugh—
I know what you mean.

She: But what did you say?

Me: I told him just that his body and brain
were part of his horn. If the story he told through
his horn—like he said—was really the big thing
in his life, he'd better start treating his body as
if it was as important as the valve seats on his
horn. I just told him about diet and exercise and
generally about uncrudding himself... you know.

She: And he cried?

Me: Yeah.

She: What'd you do then?

Me: I kind of put my arms around him, held
him for a little while, then I split, 'cause I knew
there was a guy coming over to turn him on.

Today I'm writing in the Metro station, the
only place I could find with enough warmth to
unlimber my fingers. The only place in the barren
land called Paris—Paris-Sunday, under the city,
Sorrow Sunday. Many trains come and go—people
on and off, crowding... my god! Human suffering
sometimes is more than I can bear—the brave pain
on their faces.

Just give me something, girl—I must see your
woman's strength—a word of togetherness—the sound
of you and I on your lips, the look of it in your
eye—you know I live only partly without your hand
—can't, don't want to live without you—kiss suck
fuck caress smile cover me crawl through me over me
under me chew me bite me eat me and oh love me
now, tomorrow, forever, please, what is life alone—

120

I'm looking down a dark tunnel could this be life
without you — your face. Its unbelievable sweetness,
and oh your tender touch — No, to hell with you,
girl, you're no woman — a child — a lost, helpless,
tiny child playing old worn lovers' games. Your
literary, artist Left Bank scene, your popularity!
Shove your popularity — I'm the only human being to
ever give you hope and you don't know it, can't see
it — and the grey lost world of death you love and
must feed your vein to keep. The sun warms me
through and Paris still harbors the black plague
with corners never touched by the sun and you die
here — dying — and you love it, and you embrace your
death. O leave, girl, go — get out — insanity — take
the needle out of your arm and let me fill you with
seed and swell with life, our life — I offer
paradise unforeseen and your ego clings to games —
I'm wrong — again I'm wrong — is there, could there
be greater terror than death-life, alone-life, no-
together? Your forlorn melancholy world and the
sweet shadowy figures stirring through — they
accept the living death of their addiction — even
hope a myth to them and you. Light your candle,
smoke your opium, run your smack — I terrify you —
I'm a life in the sun — the grey world I'd never
share — while you cry for a sweet fix, I cry for cool
sweet water — my need to feel clean, to feel — to feel
it all more — that wild, soul-quaking thing — and
the pain too — yes, even the pain — So pump yourself
through with venom, your first love — slink back to
your grey world of dullness — dull the pain and
dull the joy — The big flash — the big thrill — don't
miss the vein — hurry, I can't wait — hooked again —
No, better the blade than the needle again and
again and again. Was it true — could we have loved—
loved large enough — could I have filled its place,
filled your body and womb and veins with new life,
and could you have given me the woman's strength?

The world and its stupid "male supremacy" lie — how
short they see — a flexed arm and call it strength.
And the look in a woman's eye holds all of
everything for all time for all men — the one that
says Yes I'm yours and you are mine — the great
truth, the great strength for all men — flex, idiot —
her look — her yes — and what strength for what task
is yours, all, yes, all.

The grey world, shadow figures, the passwords —
"There is no life! — Nothing is anything!" — Man! Let's
get straight — where's the pot — the horse — the junk -
-the shit — let's get high — completely out of it —
later with the world — pass on everything. Dear one,
can't you see? The only way out of the pain is
through the pain, understanding the pain. How can
you understand what you can't feel? Feel it! Let it
out through you, the hurting. Talk to it — love it,
your friend, like all things natural it's trying to
talk to you, like all pain it's telling you its story
— listen and learn and live. No I can't promise no-
pain. Yes, the loss of one pain opens fresh wounds.
And the loss of a pain opens a fresh joy and your
days become more full, so take the needle from your
arm, weary threadbare angel, fall out of love with
junk and in love with the Truth even should it be
pain, come out of the shadow.

Look! She wouldn't, couldn't listen, it's so
hard to give up on an old love, so hard when the
new one sings a strange song, an unheard song, a
lonely song. How can he sing of hope? The fool!
Doesn't he know?... Doom — that's the story — doom for
all the poor little two-legged bastards on the face
of this crummy earth — what right to bring us a
song of joy now — now that we accept the sorrow, the
doom, and we've learned how to fix it — fix it, fix
it — fix it......... Damn you! Must I turn from you
as I turn from them? The unreasoning moronic
masses and their everyday fix of monotony, of

routine, of hate — yes I turned away. But you! The sweet one, the loving one — couldn't stand or understand your aloneness, your gentleness, your beauty — no! You didn't fall in love with your tender precious differentness and fuck society — No! You didn't stand proud and clean and sure — No! They terrify you, frighten you... to death — those unreasoning faceless masses — those impotent masses and their ubiquitous self-ennobled stupidity are too much, just too much for you. Why? Is it simply because they outnumber you millions to one... "So!" but you! No, "It's just too much, can't cut it." The world of people is a cruel hard-heeled vicious thing and it hurts and you fix the hurt. It hurts me, passing on you, turning my back on any potentially wonderful human being is rough. But you sweet one, sometimes it seems unbearable, you show me so much, you make a tone, a hue, a line of beauty, and my day comes alive. But then yes I know they're really only lovely shadows that flicker on paper, in the sudden flash-glow of the high in your veins; and the residue, your fading soul. And it saddens me so — saddens — saddens.

I must have slept well last night, can't remember being wakeful but Lee's face was the first thing that happened to me this morning. I was full of Lee, must have dreamt a poem of her, dreaming of Lee infinite eternal woman-child who needs my father strength, brother strength, son strength, lover strength, yes all of this I would be to her and more if I knew of more. How strange of me falling for a junkie. Me of California sea and sun and she of the ancient city, her veins clogged with its dirt.

Oh yes — the great truth Yes I know — listen there is no hope. No — none — no hope — never — never — alone — cold — isolated — stupid in pain — loveless — the shrinking din of dissonance pounding their

ears pressing the brain — compressing — pushing —
hands clapped to shield — trying — bodies slowly
rocking rocking rocking to and fro — rocking as at
cradle rocking and the din rising rising rising
rising — intensity of vibration — rising — sound
beyond the drum of ear — unheard — felt — yes rocking
— tearing — rending — searing — explosion — yes
explosion — ceiling smeared with lung juice — pink
and bright spots of red — the corner — feces all
tangled in chunks of colon... No I must be wrong
everyone's smiling.

The Metro trains keep coming by, and sometimes
I look up and a pair of eyes are deep into mine.
The train moves away and each time the eyes hold
as long as they may. Can I read these eyes? Can
they read mine? What if suddenly we acknowledged
these intense efforts to speak... you funny man,
why are you sad? Wait, come back, speak, just once
speak from out of your depth, open your soul — just
once — from one human being before I die, just once,
so that I will know it all meant a thing, something,
had a meaning if only a small thing even, but a
thing. Please understand, eyes deep into mine, I'm
trying, I want to — very much I want. Sometimes it's
rough, searching alone. Strange, believing in a
thing unknown to my world. Her fabulous face comes
spinning out of the Metro tunnel, out of its vaginal
blackness and grows immense and is everything all to
me, "cinemascope" — in full color too.

How can you be so wrong about another human
being — I know I'd never seen such a radical change
in a person — I knew that it wasn't true this thing
that appeared as a radical change — was no change
at all — it had always been there lying in wait
but I couldn't see it — this is terrifying it means
that you can never really know anyone — that
cannibalistic quality can just lie in wait for you
and inevitably when you're most vulnerable bang

you're gone gobbled up — I Must Remember this moment
as long as I live — Realize what an important truth
dawned on me at this time — Now I've done this before
— the above I mean and later upon reading it — the
thing seemed trite — obvious — This probably means
that it was a thing that I knew intellectually
but had never felt really felt before when I read
it later I couldn't feel it again but still understood
the thing intellectually. But when it came to me
while riding on the Metro — it was like a light
slowly turning on — it actually seemed to be getting
lighter somewhere — certainly not on the train but
inside me somewhere — I kept thinking and looking
trying to figure out where I had been blind — not
able to see Lee for what she really was — Ok I've
been blinded by beauty and sex before — but this
other thing — the sweetness — she was the sweetest
girl I'd ever known — Now her dog she loved that
dog but she knocked hell out of it — not sweet —
Opportunist — associated with people like Zena for
what she could get — not sweet — As soon as I moved
in and declared myself she turned bitchy — don't
take drags on my cigarette and many small things —
not sweet — Dictatorial no one can do anything right
— eats you out after — not sweet — Phony cutesy
accent French completely different from normal
voice — not sweet — She had absolutely no sense of
humor — not sweet etc. Her voice at times very coarse
and rough — not sweet — so there it is how many times
in my life — old friend Bob Sevier for one, you say,
"I know they're mean or vicious or whatever but not
to me — they treat me different" — maybe so — but not
for long — not for long — your day will come — The
worthwhile person's attitude is for himself and has
nothing to do with you — example: my honesty — if it
isn't working all the time then it's not a part of
them — watch out your turn will come.

Ah yes, sweet Lorrie Lee, help you I would if I could — but to be consumed, walking around with the teeth of your hurt chewing at my joy, to die on the hoof, to watch myself spat out in the blood of your heroin vomit, to sit at your feet or stand in the corner pushing myself small till you turn on or off or inside out, waiting for a glimpse of your tenderness: the feel of it in the dark room exploring my skin and the sex and the bodies and the intelligence and the completeness. My corner, my place at your feet, how small then. Ah yes, sweet Lorrie Lee, your leech has sharp teeth. I would if I could.

This is not the most important thing in my life — I'd stop writing to be with you ten minutes, ten years — if there were a you.

I remember when I came back to my French girl after my American girl turned American. I remember I ran that last block and pounded up the stairs three at a time and pounded the door and oh christ yes her eyes were full still with sweet simple candor and her arms my home.

PARIS - FRANCE

No one's ever bought it yet, but they're still out there trying—just about everyone and where I look it's like that, groaning and grinding it out for finance security and maybe even love. But if you ask 'em, they'll come up with something like "You've got to eat, boy." Well they're eating, but love they're not getting or giving much of. You know how it all started? Well, there was this guy—he's little, he's young, and he's Jewish—a fact which doesn't exactly help alleviate his like-everybody-else emotional problems. Anyway, a day he was standing in front of Schwab's Drugstore and he sees a beautiful blond drifting along Sunset in her

 fur-covered 2-seater 1958 T-Bird (if you don't believe it, come to Hollywood) and he did what they call fall in love. Now this short swarthy Semite each and every morning in his mirror looked dejectedly upon his protruding proboscis. She was prettier than he... obvious; and the need of a compensatory measure... obvious. Nobody loves a Jew—you and I may not feel that way but he knows better, they've been telling him sheenies and kikes were no good since he was an embryo. Hell yes, he got the message long before he could understand the words; and who is he? No great brain, no deep well of understanding, just a guy who wants to be loved, and he feels inadequate...

HOLLYWOOD - USA

He is inadequate! Two ways he can go: one, to become
adequate, warm and deep in human understanding
and rich in self-worth; or two, he can surround
himself with things and become worth a lot of (a
funny bit, I mean the one: "See that guy, he's worth
fifty grand") money. Of course he picks the gadgets—
obviously that voluptuous-vulva in the fur-bearing
T-Bird goes this route, and with the billboards and
TV commercials and new Hokum V8's in every garage
every year, what else?

So he becomes a talent agent and soon he's got
so many clients he's in business with Uncle Sam;
and he buys the blond and she's out fucking a male
starlet, and he doesn't care too much as long as he
can flash her around and she keeps her roots light,
and it's crazy having her pick him up at the office
and walking out with that wild tilting little ass
next to his—man is he fat and the sweat pours off
walking half a block, and he can't eat anything
solid and has to get most of his nutrition through
a straw—that's because of the duodenal ulcer and
the gas and all—and his employees hate his guts,
just like the blond, and the only thing he has
going that you could call relationships are the
guys he talks business with and it's a tiring game—
they're so avaricious you know—or around his pool,
and they want a favor or his food or to get wet or
make the blond and she's a lousy lay and besides
his copulatory organ doesn't work so good now—in
fact the only way he can go, really, is with a dyke-
type hustler who for a C-note brings her dildo and
they manage to work out something with that, and
once in a while he even makes it.

Funny! You know, when this had-it guy was
young and starting out, all he wanted was love.
Perhaps if he hadn't been Jewish... cause these
dear, way-back-gentled, deeply emotionaled people
have more problems with the money-love thing than

most — the more they're persecuted, the more they
racially perpetuate this, to them, quasi-valid buy-
love comedy.

Work + $ + stuff = happy days... erection + girl
equals ball... roman candle plus saddle equals
moon... 4+4 = 6 1/2

I see no essential difference between a
horse show and a beauty contest.

L.A. is TV Land, the skyline is nothing but
antennae. I'll tell you this, it is bigger than I am
— I've watched shows they couldn't have paid me to
go see; it's such an insidious degenerating influence,
I want to stay away from where it's wig-washing.
Will get you if you don't watch out.

My mother said to me, Henry Miller said to
me, Jesus said to me, Look at the Light.

They gave a stripper, Candy Barr, 15 years in
Texas for one joint of marijuana. A friend of mine,
here in L.A., got 5 years for one joint. U.S. penal
sentences run very long — much longer than in most
other countries. People from abroad are surprised to
find a man getting five years for a routine theft
that might get him six months in Sweden or France —
or six years for a small forgery which would merely
call for a fine in England.
Do you understand this? The most vile thing in
the U.S. is to threaten the society — to hell with the
individual who's maybe down and desperate, whatever.
American society is based on the subjugation of the
individual — the economy is geared to mass tastes
and the economy *is* America. If you don't want a new
car every year — or a pink refrigerator when white
ones are out of style — or maybe you don't even want

a car — your not wanting, is threatening to the
economy. Suppose this type of thinking should
spread and people began growing fond of their old
appliances and cars — it could be the end of the
most gigantic mass-production machine of all time —
the end of the tremendous manufacturing dynasties —
who *are* the economy — who *own* the politicians who
govern — and so the end of the U.S.A. as we know it —
the end as a world power. Tycoons and politicians,
with power gone, would have to get their love by
giving love — get good sex by giving good sex. If
they could have accomplished these things in the
first place they would have had no disproportionate
need for the superficialities of money or power. And
the expending of precious time — life time, for the
acquisition of nothingness would have been laughable
— yes, laughable to *them*.

I never buy my sex, but I know many so-called
great men who do. I know a guy — he produces motion
pictures — I remember we were driving down Laurel
Canyon one night and he was saying "No, you're
wrong Wulf. You can own people. I know — I've bought
and sold quite a few in my time." And he had — I
knew it was true. We stopped at a Strip drive-in for
a sandwich and I looked in his eyes and I could
see it — he had never been smiled at or looked on
with love — with all the stupendous stupidity of his
being he had never known love, never made love to
a girl who wasn't fucking his wallet. That poor
simple son of a bitch had no idea what life was all
about — but he had money, and power, and a Cadillac,
and a swimming pool — of course his pictures stink —
as does everybody involved in the making of them
and the vast mass of people, his appreciative
audience.

A hot Hollywood late summer nite, just goof-
driving and then following all those death-sound

130

police and ambulance wails, out past the Strip
where Sunset winds loose and fast and criss-crosses
others. When I got there, the dog was whimper-
running around in circles. The way his body was
flat and broken, I suppose that was all he could
manage. More cops pulled up. One shot him quickly.
I looked in the window. It had been an expensive
coupe. The coat she was wearing looked as if it
might be mink. You couldn't see her face the way
her head was turned with that freight-car-like
overturned refrigerator truck pressing her and with
the long auburn hair cascading down like that. I
watched a thin line of blood, incredibly red against
the white skin under those powerful searchlights —
it moved down her arm — diagonaled across the back
of her hand — stopped, and began to gather around
the band of her ring — big, a diamond — and with
those lights moving, throwing brilliant blue
flashes that ran back and forth across the twisted
instrument panel. The fluid broke over its dam; the
stone became a ruby. Her liquid life moved on —
found and lost itself on the polished fingertip —
hung for a moment, gathering — plunged down — it
kept gathering, plunging, gathering, plunging,
over and over. I couldn't look away. The lovely line
of her arm, and the death, the graceful curve of
her fingers, and the death — the dramatic contrast
of colors, and the death, held me in their beauty —
it was a Dali surrealistic composition, only more,
much more.

One of the lights changed direction. In the
agitated shadows her arm moved. A woman, over my
shoulder, moaned, "My god, she moved, I saw her." I
turned, relinquishing my ringside seat, forcing my
way through the curious.

I noticed they were beginning to cut through
to her with their acetylene torches. She couldn't
have cared less.

Hollywood: the land of fuck.

Right out of F. Scott Fitzgerald's Europe,
collecting double-takes when it red-streaked between
Sunset traffic. What an easy car to love; my SS-90
Jaguar: right-hand drive, one and a half turns from
lock to lock, big knock-off wire wheels, those gigantic
headlights, long low louvered hood. A vicious
looking son-of-a-bitch. A brutish-functional-let's-go-
esthetic-aluminum-steel poem. Tough car. Here I am,
bookmaker, loaded at the time and psycho, car
flippy, with two Lincoln Continentals, a Ford
Roadster hot rod, a Caddy with buttons for pushing
the seats and all — then I see this most Jaguar, far
far classic, next thing it's in the family. Think I
was hooked on cars? Perhaps a little insecure...?

I'll tell you this, my first day back — my
beloved Lookout Mountain Road — gentle — twisting
each turn a new full color shot — the quaint houses —
rococo mansion out of Hollywood's roaring flamboyant
past. The wild abandon of trees tall and reaching —
green the hills — splashing the blossoms and flowers
— rain warm soft-sound lulling — gutters full — water
madly down to Sunset gurgling and talking. Can you
feel it — that's my wish for you to feel — know this
thing I'm feeling my first day with my love — back
from the cities. Oh! Profane — those cities — just the
soothing quiet-room for love — room for life and
quiet and greenness and space — "but telephones are
so convenient — time-savers." Sure nothing like a
telephone for getting things done when busy or
exploding in your ear in the middle of an orgasm.
You must know the importance of the physical
surroundings that you ask yourself to function
within — the transition from city to green space —
free skies — earth rich living earth — Yes — cement
slab life No. How very very lovely — how tranquil —

to walk alone to these things after cities — city
after city. Life — there is life here — breathes into
me as I move through it — the city sucked my life
for its own as some people do — yes, some people are
like cities — no vitality — life of their own — they're
like blotters — suck your life juice. Can you even
a little grasp the significance the fantastic
importance of surrounding yourself with growing
things.

In America did you know it's illegal to be
broke — just walking empty-pocketed they put you in
jail. Weird.

It's hot. The traffic is heavy — Hollywood
Boulevard is loaded, crawling with cars — the
exhaust fumes are stifling. The signal says STOP,
we stop — the signal says GO, we go — the sign says
LEFT TURN ONLY, we turn left, the sign says NO
RIGHT TURN, we go straight — STOP — GO — TURN —
CAUTION — GO SLOW — SPEED LIMIT — FREEWAYS, GO FAST
— insanity of course, we are all demented.
The old timer told me of his "remember when"
Hollywood. "Why, the Boulevard was nothing but a
dirt road. A muddy mess in the winter — hard, rough
in the summer." So it was uncomfortable, inefficient.
So it's comfortable now? Efficient? Who's kidding
who? Progress? The mud, the roughness, without the
dictatorial signs and the congestion — which? The
conditioned robots don't care — they love it, dig
having their buttons pushed — Reisman's sign-reading
outer-directed robots — oh well.

I see the Great God Greed crouching over the
city, regurgitating, and puke fills the street
canals, climbs the hillsides — the man-maggots
wallow in the vile slime stench — immersed in
vomitgreed they become this in time — as all life

absorbs its medium. The sea wind vainly attempts to breathe clean the festering sky. The Great God Greed regurgitates again — I crawl out of the slime and taste the sunlight, the fresh breeze, my lungs happy again, and with new strength I walk away. Last-looking back I see the Great God Greed convulsively emptying itself, writhing, doubled gutter-spewing over Los Angeles... the city of the angels.

You ask me to value a society that adulates movie stars?

You can change, really — purposely, creatively. Sitting in a bar with a friendly beer reminds me how great it is to be a "wheel" — "The guy's really making it" thing. A few do; it's good to be one of the few. So at 26, with devious money, I buy a night club; and soon I'm one of the local kids who's made it, and digging it all like mad. Shiny sharp-draped, careful black moustache and all-year sunlamp tan — nothing missing. O very cool. And good thing — hiring great musicians like Howard McGee; his trumpet up close to Diz's during the wild frantic bop-time. And big, Gene Norman MC'd benefit for Charlie (Bird) Parker just coming down from a heroin-wig-out at Camarillo and the air so thick with pot-smoke (that was '46) all you'd do is walk in and you're contact-high. And it was fun goofing, balling the Earl Carroll show girls and Florentine Gardens dancers — God! I really go back, don't I? A good time, for then — and all of it still there waiting, the big fast money, the rackets, the suave assuredness. Regret none of it — part of growing, but trivial tedious now. It began boring and I hot-potato dropped it, and that's the thing... not to get rutted in. A thing is good as long as it's good — a kick is good as long as it's a kick — you can change, really.

So, ok, I have a license for the dog, the car,
the trailer, to drive, to fly, and now, my one and
only, flower of my heart, they ask me to buy a two
dollar license for you. If they need two dollars
I'll send it, but there will be no fucking-license
tacked over my bed. No, they have gone too far, my
love-life is my own affair.

With my symmetrical lawned 90-degree cornered
bourgeois upbringing, I'd felt compelled to try
marriage twice, but never again would I take my
love to an eight-to-five city clerk so some adam's-
apple-bobbing, state-sanctified, close-buddies-with-
the deity type could OK legalize my love and I. At
what a fantastic price in human dignity, to receive
the paternal head-pat of those who understand things
that should not be questioned... Sure!

I threw my clothes in the corner... My sensual
summer nite came through the window... Caressing
me... Touching my body... Wooing me... Soon I rose,
went out into her soft darkness... We made love till
the dawn drove her away.

God Bless America, the land of the free and
the home of the brave.

The years have come and gone and still I see
them — still blind, still deaf, still speeding,
rushing by. I see that nature in her evolutionary
wisdom has shorted the legs to fractional utilitarian
stubs — their heads and bodies are one shape like
clean eggs — enormous eyes and residual nose and
diminutive mouth and nothing has changed. They
still work at the ad agency, read Life, drive the
Cad, lay the substitute film star, watch TV. Nothing
has changed. They're guided now by some kind of
radar and thought-wave transmitter and pacified by
rational drugs. Huxley was right, called the shots —

"A gram is better than a damn." Don't be frightened
really, nothing's changed, they were always robots,
but so inefficient. Directed by TV commercials,
speeches, comic strip plots and the like. This much
more precise. Wonderful. Incredible how man
progressed. As I walk away seeking the sound sight
and smell of life I look back, and yes, there they
go still in their mass-made suits and frocks, still
blind, still deaf, still speeding, rushing. The
years come and go. Nothing changes.

I think it's very nice that God is pro-American.

Georgette told me she couldn't stand Americans,
but me very much she liked. Of course you get this
all the time in Paris, with the ostentatious,
pompous-walleted tourists hamming loud-mouthed up
Champs Elysees and whenever and wherever standing
out undisguiseable. Really, summertime — it's so
loaded with Hawaiian-shirted, white-topped-shoed,
and all squareville types and school teachers; most
Parisians flee to the Riviera if they can anyway at
all swing it. I told her I had no country. "Nationalism"
— the whole idea of identifying with a national
cultural or political outlook was for the simple-
minded; that the only flag I'd kneel to would be
one for human understanding; and even if somebody
came up with one, it would get departmentalized and
bureaucrated by the first psychopathic power-happy
group that came along needing a lever. I don't
think she understood, really, but she accepted me
as a man not a group member anyway.

The streets are strangely quiet. Why, what is
this? An almost ominous silence after other cities —
"No unnecessary honking of horns." Time marches on —
progress. (A natural phenomenon — French belligerence
and the machine age. Strange-sounding little horns

and Paris cabdrivers — music to the ears of Parisians, world travelers, and songwriters.) A flourish of a pen — an edict — the thing is done. I bow to your logic. Quiet Please, Hospital Zone.

The key is a big brass affair with a heavy brass number-tag attached; it looks very old and worn — the lock looks very old and worn, and the door, and the building, and the streets, and the city are all very old and worn — with the wind, and the rain, and the sun, and the grime of centuries upon them — and *there* is the beauty of Paris, its dirty, mellowed antiquity. You might laugh if you've never seen it when I tell you of the loveliness in its decay — the statues everywhere, in the parks, atop buildings, green with the corrosion and decay of metal — the buildings and the stone sculpture upon them are black and white and all the imaginable grey-shades between — the white: the rain of centuries, trying in vain to wash clean; and the black: its defeat. How many years of accumulated dirt to soften the ostentatious white stone. I know what many Americans would do, given the power — wash it, scrub everything down with violet-scented soap — paint it, get the crumby city livable, sanitary — dynamite out the congested Latin Quarter, make way for tile bathrooms and sit-down toilets. Blast, stand clear, goodbye Paris, off with the old on with the new... Long live modern plumbing.

Probably more thinking, sensitive, artistic, aware, city-type people live here or come-and-go than any other, and they stay, and they love it; and in Paris you're a relatively rich man if you have a refrigerator; in L.A. I've friends of all classes and I've rarely been in an apartment or house without one. Believe me, Paris is no sadder because of the lack.

Really, I feel as though a thing of beauty

were stolen from me — the Paris of horse-drawn
carriages. Stop and think for a moment; can you
see it, feel it? Strange to have nostalgia for a
thing you've never known — but it's there — I feel it,
a nostalgia for the inevitably slower pace of a
machineless city.

Hansom clipclopping down the Avenue des Champs
Elysees into the always traffic jam at Etoile around
the Arc de Triomphe — but gracefully, graciously,
really luxuriously, a feeling of life. Why? Because
the horse is alive, wants to go or doesn't want to
go, but he's alive. Hell! I rarely ever see anyone
pedaling a bicycle, they all have little motors
bolted to them — or the locust swarms of motor
scooters; they snort, and snarl, and stink, and
smoke up the place. Me! I'll take horse shit. But o.k.,
it's all over and I know it. Tolerate it? Dig it
some? Perhaps, but don't tell me refrigerators and
TV and Cadillacs are making life a fuller thing...
please.

Look! I'm not against technology, the advances
made possible in surgery alone warrant its acceptance
by any but a fool, but neither myself nor anyone
I've known or read has been able to surmount the
push-button. It can only be a good thing, healthy
in our lives when we are so well-oriented, so full
with self-love that nothing surmounts us. Then the
buttons can augment our lives, not become our lives.

The principle of handing down information
and technique — man utilizing one of his greatest
powers for growth and survival — jungle poison-berry
information to aerodynamics — Man the Beautiful.

The thing is that Frenchmen are accepted with
a delightful (for them) fervor in the U.S.A., which
country feels its real or imagined cultural
inadequacies, to the point of anything European
being buyable — and acquisition of a thing old-

world, like "accent," being a good good point—all accents being cute, charming, and a guy with one is a bed-cinch. A real social score, flashing anything European-voiced around the group, so Frenchmen swing in U.S.A.

Of course there is always the thing that at home a Frenchman is just the guy she grew up with, but it's more than just that; like all of us, they can't completely deny their conditioning no matter how tall in stature they go, and their little-voice tells them that girls are something like property, or nice domestic pets, and you don't let them reason, and man is king... that style bullshit. Even for an enlightened Frenchman it's a tough thing to kick, and of course she-people with the same instinctive rebelliousness and mind potential, are drug—they want to spread their lovely wings and fly the self-expression way... Flying's fun but difficult with someone's foot on your neck, even a loving one.

You know all peoples are not the same, the ethnic thing can't be denied, each culture has its Machiavellian and saintlike ones, but also each has its individual hue, its own conditioned, colored-glass viewed-through world and this same tint-glass is a constant, common obscurant, before the eyes of each member, irrespective of his degree of growth. American women have had their emancipation for awhile and they are sadsick with not really wanting it or believing it... yet. But the American males have accepted at least the idea of an equality, and when they turn the light of this upon an enlightened, life-hungry French girl, she's liberated—then she soars, and it's pretty to see.

Funny how uncool these French dancer showgirls are. If they're interested in you, they smile and talk to you, the Vegas and Hollywood girls, you

never know — there's no way; even sexing with 'em you
don't know what's happening behind those shut-me-in-
shut-you-out eyes. Reminds me of Celine one night
after the show, late soliloquizing the lines of a
French tragi-play, and how you could feel all her
way-back-since-childhood hurts, all accumulated,
one-packaged identified into the characterization —
the playwright's sad lines and Celine's bottomless
sadness were one — and it was real, how real it
was! — and we both end up crying, that's how real.
And how many Hollywood actresses I've read lines
with, and that dykelike who-could-believe-it movie-
queen bit they come on with, and how it used to
scare me — I never could find the woman in there —
what a lonely feeling. And it really terrified me
before I began meeting European chicks around
town, and still I didn't know but suspected that
possibly those "Look Ma, they talk" mannequins were
not my fate — and Big, what a free wild off-the-
ground feeling — that "these are them, take 'em or
leave 'em" sentence revoked.

Now I know of the thing, I often see it
really, in never before suspected places — like
European actress Hedy Lamar; acting-wise she never
said too much, but how strange! I see her playing
one of those straightforward ingenuous types and it
came through, and I believed it. And I've seen all
kinds of Hollywood-girl-picture-people do this and
always liked it, and it was cute. But this new
cognizance doesn't show me cuteness... no — more of a
simple, uncomplicated belief in their uterus and
womb and its joyous worth. A quiet "O that, of
course" type thing, like the early Ingrid Bergman.

You know, I'm telling you of the end of the
battle-of-the-sexes, which tragedy they build movies
and TV quiz shows ever and ever about, and
perpetually continue a sad thing. Bastards? No —

sadly tragic wheeldeal people.

Gee I'd like seeing the "good life" feeling
spread; and it could easy, when people, lots of
them, dig the validity in their true expression, and
with it that great animal arrogance glows and flows,
booms out. And fat pride and love for his species
and self, to be a member, part of it all. And with
who and what, he and she and they are, why then,
next stop moon; a great big ball on that ball, with
way-deep natural adventurous and inquisitiveness
calls and urges boing filled, 'cause it's good, and
not running from self and kind, but going for the
going. . . Yes. . . Yea. . . Wild.

Once after leaving Celine at the Moulin Rouge
I stopped in a small book shop at Place Clichy and
for fifty centimes pick up a used paperback and I'm
reading about the Chicago trial and conviction of
some guy the media's calling "The Lipstick Killer"
and it's one of those stories that really riles me
up. Here's a seventeen year old kid who, they said,
killed two women and a child — anyway they gave
him life for doing it. The court psychiatrist's
report on the boy said apparently no one has
ever had a close confidential relationship
with the boy, certainly his parents did
not. Does this say anything to you? Never
close, never confident — no never with
anyone. The poor little bastard, after
the example his mother and father
set for him, what reason did he
have to think such a thing
possible? The possibility of
feeling close to another —
one whom you could
confide in, have
confidence in, who
would try to
understand, but
how many of
us ever find
such a
thing in
another

143

person? Very few. Simple, there are very few such
people. And mothers and fathers are people and most
are so concerned with their inner problems, so full
of concealed self-hate, so busy with the necessity
of emotional concealment — protecting the soft inner
core so that they might survive, just survive — that
for a child to ask them for help with emotional
problems is ludicrous.

Look! If the first time this kid, this
"Lipstick Killer" was picked up for burglary and
upon finding that he stole for sexual excitement...
perhaps if one, just one — but no, not one soul, not
one thing that calls itself a human being; who was
his mother or father or a policeman or a newspaper
writer or reader — no, not one who had enough
initiative or academic knowledge to know the kid
was sick came forward to help or find help for the
boy. But wait — the payoff. Not one leather-assed
psychiatrist — no, not one canceled out a daily hour
to a mink coat or said to hell with the new
Cadillac and tried helping this pathetic kid. No,
I'm not talking of those who didn't understand what
fantastic pressures had to be at work inside the
boy... but those who knew and turned backs...?

So the knowing segment of society turned its
back and two women die and someone's child — a little
girl, gets cut-up in chunks and suddenly America is
interested. Interested hell! Indignant, lusting for
revenge, frightened. And they pick up the kid, beat
him a little, he confesses. They give him life.
Escaped the chair — to the bitter disappointment of
many I know — by making a deal: confessing. But what
did he confess to? What did the confession amount
to? Confessed to being a homicidal schizophrenic.

Now get this! The court appoints a group of
psychiatrists to find if the boy is insane... *Insane!*
What the hell is their story? This kid kidnapped a
little girl, cut off her head, arms and legs and

scattered the members of her body through the city
sewers and they want to know if he's insane... *They're*
insane! The whole damned world is insane. Really,
they seriously asked the doctors to examine the kid
to see if when he chops up people — he's OK. And they
all play out the scene with straight faces.

And this thing goes on and on, year after year
in our enlightened era. And some get indignant
when after Hitler and the time they burned a cross
on the lawn of the first black family in my
neighborhood, I said "I have no hope for the human
race" and I haven't. For individuals, for those
scarce, scattered, lovely, lone thinkers... Yes...
Hope, love, all I can give. But for Reisman's "Outer-
directed mob" nothing but a little, healthy, self-
preservatory fear.

By the simple statement: "I don't think you
are telling me the truth, it isn't necessary for
you to lie to me" — if you say this with quiet
sincerity and compassion — in time they will begin to
realize your wanting of the truth is not so that
you can use it against them, hit them over the
head with it, or find their soft spot, their point
of vulnerability. No, only to know them. You want
to live with them and help, but you can't till they
stop playing masquerade party with you. And yes...
yes, of course, by example and really when you
stop the diplomatic, tactful, insipid lying, life
becomes so much simpler. No longer is there a need
to remember who you are — to whom you are what — to
whom you are who — and, oh well, you know. And so
simple just to be unashamedly honest and perhaps
you won't be involved in the forming of a homicidal
psychopath. How great... you're always yourself to
everyone — very relaxing after a life-time of hide
and seek.

I think one of the most wonderful ramifications

of this principle is that you find suddenly you
have no need to surround yourself with symbols of
self-worth. No need for accumulating expensive time
and energy consuming junk; advertising to the
world "Look Mommy I'm a good boy, I drive a T-Bird —
look everyone I made it, I live in Beverly Hills."
No... no more need of prestige places and prestige
junk: because now who and what you are is obvious —
it's stated in the tone and content of your words —
it's stated in the way you walk and move and drive
a car and make love... Yes, most everyone I know
lies in everything they do — even in bed; it's
amazing the deceit practiced in sex. I know, I was
something of a genius at the game, but the important
thing about all this honesty stuff is that it
works... it pays off, it follows the fundamental law
of life, of nature, of the research laboratory...
You must start with a true premise, to arrive at a
true deduction... and its antithesis... If you begin
with a false premise, you end with a false conclusion,
a false relationship and you create madmen. This
kid, this killer was never set an example of a true
premise — never an example of truth. He was a
Catholic; went regularly to church — but the way
they presented Christ's words to him — so distorted —
a nice fairy story but nothing that he or Christ
could have applied in their daily lives.

They gave him... tact, diplomacy, subtleness,
devious means, applied psychology. They were... cool,
clever, cunning, lying, stealing, cheating. They
showed him... parent against child, lover against
lover, man against man, nation against nation and
perhaps world against world and there is no end. No,
never an end to the list of criminals and crimes.
And why? O great beautiful heaven why? Who are they
shunning — hiding from — plotting against? Each other...
Yes, each other. The poor simple boobs. Don't they
know? They have nothing else — only each other.

There is no fear in a blade of grass.
No, no fear in a tree.
No, nor in a leaf that breaks loose and
follows the wind.
There's no fear in a wild animal.
No unrealistic fear.
Their fear is true.

Some think I'm impervious, without too much
depth, that my joy and hurt flick on and off like
a theatre marquee. Like when Joli, my much-loved
German Shephord died; I was completely broken up —
and next day life is pretty again. Or my love and I
part and I come-apart; and on the way home a lovely,
little lass aphroditing down the Strip moves me.

Look, I don't carry that grief around, letting
it feed on me anymore. Hell, I used to — it could be
perhaps years to come back together again after some
emotional upheaval.

To escape into your pain, dramatize it, live
with it, for it — kind of glamorous, especially
walking around with a shroud of lost-love wrapping
your poor, forlorn, emaciated form. And that's all
right too if you feel it really, but when it's over —
drop it. And amazingly, when you just let the grief
have its way with you, let it wail — it spends itself
and goes away and lets you alone for new grieving-
growing.

It's just as much of a sin to be stolen from
as to steal, to be lied to as to lie, to be cheated
as to cheat, to be deceived as to deceive. It takes
two to perpetrate a hoax, the con-er and the con-ee,
one can't exist without the other. Are you going
to tell me that it's less stupid and unaware and
unknowledgeable to be insensitive to the con when
it is on, than to be the con man yourself, No!

I can see that: abstractions and subtleties

are beginning to bore me. I can see that: this
alienates me intellectually. I can see that: my
thinking has one chord: mind-body-soul survival. I
can see that: it's true of everyone, only a matter of
planes. I can see that: all the novelists have read
their Kraft-Ebbing and I'm tired of case-history
fiction. I can see that: the trouble with categories
is that, like astrology charts, everybody most ways
fits all of them. I can see that: most people get
their philosophy from popular songs. I can see that:
to live each day as though it were the last, is a
little short-sighted. I can see that: language is
generally more of an aid to disguise than a tool of
communication. I can see that: mice probably think
flying bats are angels. I can see that: a highly
developed objectivity leads to true subjectivity. I
can see that: the movies and the zoo show the
beautiful animals and leave me with the same
feelings of wonder and sadness. I would rip the
cages apart — but No I don't own or rule the world
— just understand it — only...

    I can see that: instinct is genetic memory. I
can see that: I'm much too soap-boxy and uncool for
the status quo. I can see that: you'll never know
what I know till you know it too.

    Seems I can see quite a bit. But to be able to
see a thing doesn't necessarily indicate that it will
manifest anything. Many times my life is a blurry
obscure thing and I accept the inevitability of
this. Until I did accept the fact that my visions
were not realities — I was lost — the constant tragedy
of perfectionism... Yes.

    To know a vision that approximates to you
perfection; to strive for, live for that vision is a
beautiful thing... A sinister thing it becomes, upon
demanding its realization... There are of course —
no absolutes in nature. An absolute, or perfection,

is an end, a total result, the sum achievement and this can't be applied to life. For everywhere nature is evolving, becoming more efficient, reaching higher to the sun, pushing deeper into the earth. Never to touch the sun — but reaching. So long as you understand the ideal realization can never be expressed; so long as you realize the working towards, the effort to become more perfect is the very essence of life — obvious everywhere to living things, this evolutionary reaching for perfection — you are in-tune with a basic Life-law... and perhaps there could be harmony.

By now you should know the truth... The anguish there: lurking behind all those smiling, those calm, those reassuring faces. Never! Not once have I grown to know another intimately, that I have not discovered the anguish there, there behind the disguise. The terror there, the real, the wild-eyed terror. Their faces in pillows wet from tears — weeping alone. Sweet Truth if all the crying alone were laid end to end; but for the rules they strive to be brave, present a good front, carry on, play the game — and everyone knows, but not really... Really can't believe *their* secret pain could be true of another: Ah the world itself would weep — can't believe because of the smiles I think — the everywhere fixed smiles, I think. So they go, go on alone — smiling brave. And cry alone, in the pillow alone, against the wall alone — wiping the tears, blowing the nose, a little shrug, a faint smile... and they die alone.

If you look into my face, into my eyes, if you say "Why so serious, why so sad?" That is why — I know the anguish inevitable. I am looking through the smile; it's a trick I know, that had to be learnt so as not to be tricked by calm and smiles... I can only love you — knowing you.

Oh, yes, I love the smile: sweet, tender,
brave, brazen, tragic thing — love it too, but to
love really, is to Know. Yes, by understanding
others, you can learn to understand yourSelf. By
understanding yourSelf, you learn to understand
others. There is no one way, no best way, only all
ways to understanding... And no other way *but*
understanding.

The merchant princes they lie they steal they
cheat all in the name of business-survival —
survival of the fittest — it's business they say and
everybody shrugs the shoulders — it's business — in
the name of business what crime is sinister,
Machiavellian? What are they lying for and
cheating for stealing for? — security a place in the
sun and respect — adulation and, ah, yes love.
Sacrilege — mentioning sweet love on the same
page as the money-man in the same book — in the same
world, but children he is — he does exist and he is
in you and I so we must look at him — look at him as
though he were some grotesque monster pulled up from
the depths of a sea and he's green, money green.

Random selections from my Dictionary of
Pornography: I'm only human; Capital Punishment;
Municipal code #780,958,321,684,9300001; I only did
my duty; Standard Oil; Muzak; Vice Squad; The
Legion of Decency; It's a question of ethics; Pure
Food and Drug Administration; Congressional Medal
of Honor; Keep off the grass... really it's too
depressing to go on. And really, anything "life"-
graphic, they'll preface with, "porno." And really
I'm such a fool and it hurts till I realize it's
relative. And really, the most precious thing they
can give you is their love for themselves. And
really, most don't have the time, they have such
full empty-lives... And, oh, is there a meaning in

this tangled pile of words.

I hate her. She is beautiful: all soft and white and green-eyes with touches of pink at the ears. While I'm reading, she comes and asks to be stroked — asks for love and I give it. But now I hate her, hate her feline whine, groveling at my feet, begging me to open a stupid can of putrid smelling crap so that she can fill her gut. I'd love to kick her across the room and I'm ashamed — the poor thing, the poor thing's hungry, why shouldn't it cry. What's wrong with me, am I some kind of insensitive beast, a thing of no feelings that I should resent the hunger-cry of this pink and white fluff-ball? No. Then why these feelings of resentment?

I resent its dependency upon me. I resent what we've done to such creatures. I resent domestication. She has sharp teeth, strong legs, keen senses, beautiful well-coordinated killing instincts — a lethal machine for death, fleet and swift and graceful in action, unself-consciously perfect in relaxation, single-minded in desire. Why then does this relatively flawless piece of life, this lovely living machine for survival, for perpetuation of its kind, grovel at my feet — degrading Nature for a can of evil smelling slop? Here kitty!

Because we are gods among animals and we are sick with it... We take them from the sea, the sky, the forest, the desert and bend them till they break and crawl on their stomachs, crawl in homage to our bilious god egos. Steal them from the fecundating wilds, where the winds are full with living scents — imprison them in sterile coffin cities of concrete and plastics where the air is a chemical, where sometimes they run for days looking for a piece of wet earth or a blade of grass and sometimes go mad with the now unanswerable call of life — of instinct.

These, the fortunate, the survivors join us in
our mutual degradation... Come kitty, here's your
can of "Pure Purr" catslop — now eat it all, the TV-
Man said it was good for you... That's a good kitty!

It all depends on what you think man is
doing to the earth; obviously technical progress
will never cease — an inevitable result of man's
instinctual curiosity. Practically anything that
can be imagined, can and will be accomplished in
time by my fellow man. Name it... A million miles
an hour, planets not even imagined in our solar
sky, whole cities hermetically sealed and on and on
and on.

And here's a guy who loves machinery born
and raised with it, can't keep his hands off. Gets
real pleasure from driving a well-balanced machine,
feeling the logic in its design, its precision response
— working on it.

But there is a thing that I know — really
know to be True. If I'm alive twenty years from now,
driving a then well-made machine and of course
enjoying it... Tell me — is my pleasure any greater,
am I enjoying the machine more? Is the moment more
important? When I go to my modern machines of
twenty years hence, do they give me more life? Do I
enjoy the ride through my city more? Do I enjoy the
foods the technology-of-future preserve and cook for
me more? Will I enjoy Huxley's "Feelies" more than
Chaplin or Cinemascope, walking by a moon canal
more than a stroll by the Seine, the feel of chemical
fabrics more than cotton or wool, a super atomic
explosion more than a blockbuster? No — I don't
think so.

When I think of my life twenty years ago
and the technology that surrounded me — I was no
happier, no sadder. When I read history or talk to
my grandfather, I see they were no happier or

sadder because of living in a particular era of
mechanical evolution. If you think I'm crusading
for a cessation of this thing, you're nuts.

The earth bouncing under my feet as a jet
cracks — sound always awes me... the majesty of
man... the animal paragon. But like wow! — there *is*
a point of diminishing-returns and the explosions
are really quite beautiful but they melt your
eyeballs.

I'm selling my motorcycle — it's very nervous,
goes too fast, passes too many interesting things
and people — feet are here to stay — who the fuck
wants a Stanley Steamer — who the fuck wants a
flighty stallion. All very nervous.

She: Is this the same phone as Hank's downstairs
in the studio?

Me: Yes, it's an extension.

She: Has the same number and when it rings
up here, it rings down there?

Me: Yes, when I answer it, if he's wanted I
stomp on the floor; the other way, he pounds on the
ceiling for me.

She: How high is his ceiling?

Me: Not very high, he reaches it easily (I reach
up and pound on air) about this high — it's a low
ceiling.

She: Why don't you put in a bell? Then you
could ring each other!

Me: It would be just something else to go
wrong — I like to keep it simple. Anyway, like this
we can feel each other; a stomp on the floor or a
rap on the ceiling can have a feeling of life — you
can say quite a bit.

A bell! Shit.

I don't know what they expect from it all! I
don't know of anyone who was delivered with a

warranty for happiness, or even what is meant when
they speak of it; I get the feeling, to most people
it pictures a kind of blissful condition with
everything warm and billowy and tranquil — with
perhaps a not too violent orgasm once in a while.
Are they right, with their claims of an unconscious
retrogressive wish for the black gooey locked-door
womb state? Interesting — that indefinable state
called happiness.

For me, I know that, in a way, the possibility
of it, of happiness, began one day while walking a
deserted path in the hills above Hollywood... My
moment... my little piece of time and space, seemed
to stop so that I might capture it — and simply — no,
gigantically this little hunk of frozen time was...
all... everything... as much as I could expect of
life. And as I stood there; though nothing changed
in dimension or hue — no, the same, but now all
intensity and significance. The trees and flowers
and grasses and weeds and all... A Van Gogh
landscape, each color vibrant, screaming almost with
an inner burning. And when they bent themselves to
the wind, the motions had the same quality I felt
in the colors and the wind too the same quality
and I too the same vibrancy and intensity and I
knew, really knew at last... these things and I
were one, we spoke of the same force, faced the
same destiny... we were alive together. And after a
while I began to laugh — a joyous one of discovery,
the promise of heaven answered and I couldn't hold
it all and went to write this, speak of it, to share
the new bigness with another, others.

A revelation? An instant of inspiration or
insight? No! It was at this particular point in my
time, when books I'd read, people I'd listened to,
ideas, thoughts, experiments all culminated,
crystallized themselves into a conclusion or an
attitude — becoming an integrated, definable,

expressible part of me — and so a plane of
understanding reached. This is what they call
revelation.

From that day forward, little by little,
moment by moment I've learned the wonder in living
the Instant — am still learning, always will be
learning.

Sometimes when I'm bogged down with stupid
everyday hassles, busy with being an asshole —
sometimes the lovely line of a cheek, the song in a
word, clear cool water in my throat. Sometimes these
things stop me — tell me of the simple beauty, simple
realness, simple truth. Sometimes then the business
drops off like a grotesque garment and I'm alive
again.

Yes, sitting in a café across from a friend...
a smile or thought exchanged... deep in passion
with my love... walking in the warm rain... snarl
of hate from a sad idiot. Yes, these are the things
of life. No more — no less. Each to be lived or to be
lost. For you and I — nothing more — nothing less.
Perhaps if you can come to realize this thing, these
simple small moments and acts contain all of it,
the sum total of your life. Perhaps then you'd begin
to feel the lushness and the richness in what is
called the incidental and trivial... moment.

THE ARTIST

Sobs erupt within me — the tears blind me — sobs and tears — won't stop. I want to read more — it's so beautiful — but I can't see — I roll over on my back and let the sobs run their course — let my fingers touch the print, move across it lovingly.

The story... a true one — a man's love for his artistry, his work.

The man... Frank Lloyd Wright.

The work... Imperial Hotel, Tokyo.

The time... 1915.

Earthquakes, vicious earthquakes — nothing withstands them but paper houses and these always burn in the after-fires. Tokyo needs a large multi-storied hotel — impossibility — it's fated to topple. Wright, in fearless architectural logic, says he can do it, he can float the whole damn building on the mud shelf deep below the surface... and the world laughs... keeps laughing. The building begins — the world laughing — against impossible odds — the world laughing — laughing — laughing — the building almost complete and within the sound of the laughing ridicule comes another sound... terrifying sound... ominous sound. The biggest roughest earthquake in fifty-one years. Wright and one assistant stand alone atop the building; the building built on principles unknown to the laughing world; untried in the laughing world. Known only in the purity of his art. Known only in the sweet Truth of his mind...

He called it Organic Architecture.

And while the earth and the building went
insane under his feet — and the world laughed —
Wright watched a doomed city again disintegrate into
rubble and flame. The building — his building —
shrugged off quake and flames... and stood... and
stood long after many who laughed were gone. One
of Frank Lloyd Wright's shrines to the creative
beauty of free functioning minds...

He called it Organic Architecture.

And I cry. Yes cry for the beauty in his story.
And yes it says there is only Truth, only Truth will
transcend the impossible. And yes I cry in pain
for a world cluttered with men and buildings of
no courage... no theme... no purity... no integrity.
Will I always cry for this — because of this? Yes I
think yes. Men who believe are so few... and quite
alone. Quite alone... and now they tear it down —
Hilton Forever and there are those who cry out at
this loss.

So do it — do the thing — don't be afraid —
better to be afraid not to do it — not doing it is
failing anyway — so what's to lose — do the thing —
paint your picture — dance your dance — sing your
song — build your bridge — write your book — The
important thing tell your story — this you must do,
you will do anyway — your life will be your story —
so make it big — a grand thing — you may be the
biggest idiot that ever lived — probably are but look
if you tell your story in the grand style — you are
only being efficient — the farther you call the more
often you call — the more to hear you — so paint your
picture they will come — yes they will come. They're
looking to you now — they will come — so — say this
thing you must say it as loud and as often as you
can and they come — a few or millions I don't know —

depends on who you're talking to — the few or the
many — but they'll come — can you see I'm talking of
efficiency in communication — can you deny a lecture
hall being more efficient than a cafe table — a book
more efficient than an infrequently recited poem
even if you believe in inefficiency — you're going to
get more from associating with others who also
believe in inefficiency — true? Then you must be
efficient in your denunciation of efficiency — write
a book — believers in inefficiency from every corner
they come and become your friends — nice huh? You
can even form a club — the important thing of course
in all this is being with — associating with —
sleeping with — fighting with — those people who you
feel at least some degree of compatibility — rapport —
affinity — if you don't experience this in your life —
what are you — one who spends his life in the company
of those with whom there is little or no communication
— a bad thing.

Are they kidding? They must be; apparently
intelligent human beings; making ludicrous faces,
grimacing, pointing black pistols at each other,
dousing themselves with catsup, kissing and crying,
speaking and screaming unbelievably inane lines.
No, I know they're not kidding — they're getting paid
and the hacks who give them their lines — they get
paid and those who point in the direction they
should walk and talk — they get paid; everybody gets
paid and for what? Being idiots. The young girl in
the thing I saw tonight. I met her when she first
came to Hollywood... wild body and face and she
told me she was an actress. Well honey it ain't so,
just ain't like that. But with that ass — don't
worry, you'll go far, and that's all she wants. But
some of those others in the film — that ridiculous
film — old timers, talented actors, putting up
with a shitty set-up like that. Crumby production,

creaking with incompetence; it'll make money, it was
made to make money, sure, but can't you just see
them between takes and at home in the evening,
rationalizing the whole thing to each other — to
their families.

Tell me, are swimming pools, expensive
husbands and wives, name colleges for the kids,
and what we call a high standard of living worth a
day like that? Man, I know if you have anything on
the ball at all, any pride in yourself, any integrity —
making scenes like that, I don't care what the
money is — kills you. I mean literally kills you,
drains all the sap, leaves nothing but a hulk.
You've got to get drunk or turn on or escape into a
hobby or sex or something or flip. No luck — you'll
flip anyway.

Psychoneurosis, nervous break-ups or downs;
none of the intelligent talented ones can get away
with it: 'cause they're using their talent to bore
themselves — criminal yes... Truly. The punk kids
with the build and profile of beauty contest, bod of
lush flesh — no matter no Mind; but those old timers?
After all the dues paid — amazing what these people
will subject themselves to for position, maintaining
a place in the dumb housing tract of Beverly Hills,
a Mercedes rather than a Ford, or so that they may
ride rather than walk.

Acting — what a strange profession in the first
place. Used to consider it myself, very interested
for a short time. Jimmy Dean said it was an
excellent way to work out emotional problems. Well
perhaps, though it didn't work out so well for him
and I can't see a person after True understanding,
deep knowledge of Self, one who really wants to
love him or her Self taking it seriously. I can't
see such a person choosing acting as the particular
mode of expression, the particular pursuit of Self.

Those whom I've met who had a real propensity

for it, were people whose primary need was to get out of themselves or who feel that only in this way — acting, will they be able to express the many ramifications of their personality. Not through living! Only through acting.

Obviously a person with enthusiasm for expressing life can't be bothered spending his days expressing himself vicariously through a playwright or screen writer. However if you don't feel this far-off lofty goal attainable for yourself, and you still want to act — OK, I'll tell you how to go about it rudimentarily — the only way it can be done, the way you'll do it anyway, whether you know it or not even if you Method and Stanislavsky yourself to death.

Don't be awe-frightened by the nomenclature. Forget the words particular to acting. So many vainly feel they are part of a thing, when they glib-master the vernacular. In fact, forget the word acting — there is really no such thing, you know. No, when someone turns in a great performance, they are portraying one character and that is themselves — I don't care how different from their everyday personality it seems.

You are never acting... the strength of your performance depends upon your ability to recognize and experience retrospectively the emotions and fantasies out of your past: murder, gentleness, fury and serenity, all of them you know and it is your ability to re-live what you have previously experienced and fantasized that makes what they call an actor. Obviously true — you can't express what you don't know; something does not come from nothing; you can get damned little warmth from a vacuum.

Kid actors: They know about love and hate, but those innumerable, delicate nuances between... tough.

True you might have to study ten years of dramatics — but only to accustom yourself to re-living an emotion before an audience. And that's all you'll gain from it unless they turn you into one of those mechanical characterizations, all pat-memorized from Tony the organ-grinder to Noel Coward — just wind 'em up, push the correct button and stand back.

So Barrymore's Hamlet was Barrymore; Olivier's Hamlet was Olivier and that's the way it is right down the line. Look, really — acting like any other art form is a means of expressing yourself — that's all. And every comedian and tragedian down through the years has been motivated by this same need... to express himself. Why the hell do you think they were up there on the stage in the first place? Because they love the theatre or the play?... Please. They want to be seen: They want to be heard: They want to be felt; and the play is only the vehicle, as it is so aptly called. Love for their medium — a secondary emotion, exists only as it gratifies the first.

No kiddies — you cannot learn to act. You can re-live your anguish and joy before an audience — that you can learn.

And the deeper you are, the deeper you've felt... the deeper your performance. But you — always and only you, whether you play Christ or Jack-the-Ripper — you... only you. The Secret Life of Walter Mitty — how true of most great actors. The poor unhappy miserable bastards.

Listen, at least hold out for a decent script — lines with substance. To hell with their promises; demand characters with balls or ovaries or characters truly insipid, believably insipid, people torn right out of life, people who could bleed, people who shit. Those puppet parts will kill you. God knows we need good actors; they give us much — yes. So if that's your route; go dear ones... but don't let 'em consume you.

And this guy writes fictitious stories about fictitious people, in fictitious situations, in a fictitious world... by a fictitious author. They gave him the noble Oscar. Has anyone ever passed on the whole deal or refused the tribute and asked, "just for the money please" — Beautiful.

I was insensitive enough to believe Brando might, but he was nicey-nice bland as any. Too much to ask — I suppose. But really how can you take all that pomp-mush-mouth seriously, when you look at all the no-talent clowns that have made acceptance speeches. Well onward...

I remember all night from Paris to Dunkerque; across the channel then customs at Southampton. I'm worried with banned books everywhere; inside my shirt, jammed in pockets; under my duffel-coat. I'd heard nothing but how tough they were at British Inspection, but even bulky waddle-walking the way I was, no one frisked me. So, cool... Henry Miller finally got to London.

Johnny and I sunsoaking at Von's sidewalk tables; with two movie guys writer-talking us about the industry. It seems they, like most of them, collaborate on everything they do; that way if either one of them comes up with anything creative, the other can squelch it. With these people the criteria of art is, "If it's not commercial, it's art." They said sure we're writing crap but we're still young we can play along for ten or fifteen years until we get enough money power and prestige (oh I love those words) then we'll be able to do something worthwhile. I remember after we left Johnny said "What makes them think they can overcome an additional ten or fifteen years of conformistic conditioning when the first twenty-five dried 'em out?" The capper on this — they sold the thing for two-thousand to some blob that calls itself a producer. I've met him, he has a green scum on him like any stagnant pool. Now I hear they got an attorney to watch the blob; of course they'll be busy watching the attorney, which will leave them little time for writing (do I sound bitter) but this is OK; they've got their foot in the door of the movie factory (I'm not) and there is always some simple boob who'll ghost-write — or plagiarize (It's funny a little). Of course this feeds on a thing inside, called pride or self-respect or something like that, but what the hell, a guy's got to play the game. Anyway there's always getting loaded or golf or sex — sure that's it — sex.

Reading a Truman Capote interview in the *Paris Review*. An excellent writer this Capote; writes beautifully and poetically about nothing. Mr. Capote feels that to write well the writer should expend his subjective emotional involvement with the content of his work before putting it to paper — bullshit, ask Van Gogh or Miller or Diz or Miles. These pages are covered with joy and tears... my joy, my tears; I think you know this; I know when I read someone if this is true of them. No I didn't think it was true of Capote. No it wasn't necessary to read the interview to know the man; to know the man read his work... yes read him. To me this most graphic of art forms is of course, like all art, a direct effect of the need to communicate, and writers communicate to me... oh how they communicate. How many times I've started a piece and stopped reading to throw it across the room in disgust "the insipid ass" or stopped reading as the artist fills me with the beauty and strength of his love or hate or anguish — too moved to read on, and over and over again "Oh you beauty-full bastard, you beauty-full bastard; man how I love you." Do you ever feel this — like kneeling before a canvas or book or whatever; with thank you for being; thank you for coming to me; speaking to me out of a world of deaf and dumb mutes — where a man may walk for days never hearing the sound of a human voice, or knowing the sweetness of a human ear open to good or evil... but open.

And I don't like talking to writers about writing or painters about painting. It's really ridiculous; like talking to a jazz player about his solos; it's there to see or hear or it's not, there's nothing to say — but everywhere it's the same; cliques of artists moving in close for comfort and security.

Ninety-some percent of all the art I see says absolutely nothing to me; leaves me cold; moves me not. Painting, photography, poetry, sculpting, acting, films, TV, stage, novels, music; classical, jazz, popular, folk, most of it completely junk — good to kill a few moments with, but as for it heating you or cooling you... seldom happens.

Sure I read, go to exhibits, always listening and looking and not listlessly — but the only thing that keeps it from becoming this... every so often something happens and then it was all worth it; but the shit you must wade through to get there! Funny how people are always asking me if I like poetry or movies or the like and I don't; or someone will say "Do you enjoy art?" No, I enjoy the exciting, the beauty, the ugly whenever I encounter it; whether it's in a dress some kid made for herself or the architecture of a building... it moves you or no. OK — right now I feel the futility in all this; all

this talk, this book, the emptiness out there in
you. Out of the thousands there would be only a
handful who even began to understand — and yes,
it's to the handful I look; the growing flowers,
popping up through the weeds... here and there.

To hell with it... I'm bored with eloquence
without substance; please take all of art and shove
it up your collective asses — sick to death I am of
this constant rumble and chewing and pawing the
dirt about art. Portrait painters and bullfighters —
shit — the only artist in me is the frightened little
boy. So tired I am of the angel artist, political
artist, violent artist, bed artist... I know... I
know there seems to be no other beauty emanating
from a human soul, so how can you accept such as
this... I know. Approximate the beauty of God's
nature? Fool. You are god. Your sunset, your sunrise,
your hand-wrought forms as rich with beauty as
those you call his. Eternally they perpetuate
themselves — those sunsets; and why with childish
glee you duplicate? Fool — you are the sunset —
fool... duplicating yourself.

Subject matter; what else do I want from an
artist? What you have to say is everything. If you
want to say it bad enough... you'll find a way. If
they don't make canvasses large enough for you...
you'll find a way. If there's no medium that fits...
you'll make one. What technique is necessary — new
or old... you'll develop. All of Capote's talk of
de-emotionalized, well-constructed sentences — man
there is no way to write a sentence except your way.
Oh, go back to your upholstered holes.

Thank you Kenneth Patchen — thank you Henry
Miller — you held out your hands to help — I took
them — of course they were bloody — it's always like

that when you rummage around through your own
bowels and guts searching. I won't bother to wash. I
like the color you bleed.

The Lincoln Continental Mark 1; for quite a
few years I drove one. Big — but they ride, handle
and corner like a sports car. Esthetically it had
its bad points, but compared to the average American
automobile it was outrageously beautiful. I remember
walking to it — almost invariably I got a glow from
this touch of man-made beauty in L-uglycity-A. Sheer
pleasure being transported about by a thing of
symmetry rather than a meaningless glass rubber
and steel glob. I know a thing of beauty always
stops me dead whatever I'm doing, but people in
general were incredibly immune to this car. Every
so often I'd climb in though, and someone would be
standing there just looking. I remember this one
tired looking little guy saying "You know I noticed
your car at first because it's obviously different,
but the longer I looked the more it began to make
sense. I've been standing here twenty minutes; I
suppose people think I'm nuts or planning to steal
it but somehow it feels kind of logical and I didn't
want to leave." We talked for awhile; he'd studied
art in high school; now he was selling washing
machines. He climbed back in his Detroit moon
rocket and Flash Gordon'ed off to convince the
world that buying a Super Duper spin clothes
mangler would be a glorification of the home; the
resulting exaltation cheaper than psychotherapy.
Ernst Fuchs, the Austrian painter — new to
the country — genius type, uninterested in anything
mundane. The first time he saw the Continental, "Is
that an American car? It's lovely." Another guy, a
sculptor in about the same awareness category,
remarked, "Well I see the automotive industry is
finally using creative designers." The car was

fifteen years old at the time... What does beauty
know of time?

Trouble with a book: if the writing is a living,
searching, evolving thing, it must contradict itself.
Only alternative is publishing one page at a time.

Allen writes beautiful, sad, tragic, lost
poems about people like that. Reading me — he said
"I don't like to be shouted at, talked to so much."
Then dear Allen, don't stop; let me see you look up;
understanding misery, you accept misery — but not
its pain; hurts inside so much and there's the pills
and powders and smoke and juice and life continues
misery. Shouting and talking? Hell man... maybe I
should get a big drum and a uniform.

Words upon words upon words upon words.
Shakespeare, Dostoyevsky, Melville, Hesse: grand
tragedians sounding the gigantic minor tones; their
work a great organ. They improvise the dissonances
and confusion rampant in the human mind. Gide,
Celine, Tolstoy, Rimbaud: novel after novel, imbecilic
hero after imbecilic hero, defeatist poem after
defeatist poem and on and on and on — Sweet Truth
is there no end to all this? Really not only am I
to the point where I'm fed up with talking to idiots
— I sure as hell don't want to go on reading about
them. Great talent; incredible facility with
language, ability to bring book-people alive;
beautifully finely delineated characterizations.
Look, I know it had to be said and must be repeated
and repeated and repeated and I love the great
ones for saying it, and so wonderfully. Sure
societies and their composites are many ways fucked
up... yes. And wonderful that so much genius has
chosen to great and graphically picture and dissect
the malignancies — but ever so infrequently comes D.
H. Lawrence who some understands the fuckedupness

and iconoclastically scythes it down, topples it and with the other hand says sex can be fulfilling, life can be rewarding and perhaps even talks of nobility. Yes how creative all the tearing down, if something is offered to replace the wreckage... a thing to build on. How seldom anyone who writes with a positive pen in the unending paper sea of negative literature.

"What have men to do with goals? Who spend their lives flying from themselves... their only goal." — Kenneth Patchen

He'd spent days working on the sports car —
I said, it's not the answer, it has nothing to do with living.
He said — Hell, I know it.
I looked back, and he was on his knees, and his hands in the machine —
I said — But you love singing. How can you let them make you sing this crap —
He said — Yes I love singing — love to sing.
And while I watched, they dressed him in a chartreuse suit and stood him in a chorus line.

Such a great spirit was Lawrence. A good man I'd like to have known.
And to the incessant "Why do you wear a beard?" He answered "What beard?"

Ayn Rand: *The Fountainhead* and Howard Roark, and to mention either among a group of what are known as the literati is to demonstrate an alarming, embarrassing naivete. Roark, with all of his impossible paradoxical hung-upness is one of the few fictional characters I've encountered who offered, philosophically, an iota of big-life hope to an intelligent reader. The book was a bestseller, and curious, I've questioned a lot of readers concerning its essence; only a handful had the slightest cognizance of Rand's purpose. I found they bought the book for the brutality — the violence — in the man — in the sex scenes — and I know also because of the Dick Tracy-like, comic strip stereotypeness of its characters: black and white, good guys and bad — "Meanwhile, back at the ranch..." OK — OK, corny, but goddamn it offered hope, and a kind of hope I believed in. The kind of hope in the first bit of gutty life that became amphibious, squirming out of the slime-brine; the kind of hope that every great leader/thinker from Christ down to men like Emerson has tried to put across; the only hope worth a tinker's damn on this man-drearied planet since it began its cooling... "And tuning his mind and hand to life-force; man sculpts his destiny..."

His own destiny! What a gigantic thought. Too godlike? You want to make up fairy stories and live by 'em or just beat the drum of defeat and bitch about what a shitty deal the fates dealt you... either way you're dead.

The Fountainhead was a serious effort to lead men out of the slime and I thank Ayn Rand; it was an important novel with all of its faults; and why? Philosophically creative subject matter. Show me a guy who likes a piece of writing on the basis of glib well-constructed sentences, good well-constructed entertainment, oblivious to subject matter, to content, and I'll show you a decadent ass, a literary fop (I like the sound of that — "literary fop") but really as far as I'm concerned there are very few novelists I care to talk to, which is exactly what goes on when I'm reading; I talk back in agreement or disagreement but definitely a two-way discussion; and I've finally matured to the point where I put down a piece of writing as soon as it becomes obvious nothing is being said, just as I drop out of a blabla peripheral conversation — of course I'm condemned as a crude crass individual, lacking in social finesse, tact and diplomacy......... guilty.

Since I wrote the above I've tried to read Rand's new book *Atlas Shrugged* and so very badly I was embarrassed for her; but still in a way enjoyed what I could read of it. There she was, still trying to send up flares to the world for the thing she sees as hope; but Sweet Truth how she's degenerated since the other book. I know now what killed her. I wish I could say that I saw the seed of this in her earlier work *We The Living, Anthem, The Fountainhead* but didn't, though it certainly was there... She lacked humor completely. Humor... and what is humor? "The relief-valve of accepting imperfection." Couple the inability to accept imperfection in Self, in others, couple that with an inflexible ego and rigor mortis picks up the cards.

And yes! Great-souled Erich Maria Remarque and the rough elemental dignity of "Kat" in *All Quiet on the Western Front*. And then his beautiful, incredibly human refugee Surgeon "Ravic" of "Arc de Triomphe" — Boyer and Bergman and Laughton and Calhern caught the whole thing in their poignant film: dignity, real, warm, Human Dignity — it was so full with life and love and believable death... it moved me.

We are wonderful things, we humans. The Truth of our emotions makes it so.

"To achieve the superior, you must first reject the inferior." — Frank Lloyd Wright.

"I don't see anything particularly wrong with mediocrity — everyone must do something and who can it hurt?" A question I encounter I think more than any other — so rich in blandness, so ripe with ignorance it could be the base for the mental putrefaction rotting out the minds of men.

I remember Diane and I were sitting in my Continental talking — she was defending her current sex chum — as usual he or she was the greatest living exponent of wisdom in modern times; anyway I had pointed out that while he was a talented dancer he wasn't dancing, and for an artist his life was busy busy with an incredible degree of eye-saddening line-hue-form-junk-stuff. An oil painting hanging in his living room with the numbers painted in — you know No. 1 for red, No. 8 for green, etc... sure — a modern American car in one of the more nerve-shattering designs, Brooks Bros'. suits, enough? Enough. The going was heavy, the thing was to show her that an artist with depth would not be surrounded by all this crap, and a sensitized one could be destroyed by it. She replied it wasn't important, these things were of no real consequence in a person's life — even writing words like these I shudder.

We were parked on Hollywood Blvd., talking, before going into a coffee shop. I looked around: an example? Easy, essence is everything, and there it was across the street, an old office building out of Hollywood's fabulous days, grand in rococo, and around the top a hundred or so cast-concrete angels or cherubs like do-di-dads, perfect, too horrible for anyone to accept. We both sat there letting our indignation rise against these little concrete celestial-kids, this affront to any acceptable line the building may have had. I began to tell her of the many many man-hours that went into those little angels. First someone had to sculpt these atrocities, molds made, concrete poured, specially-skilled

workmen to fix them in place — much time and effort
and nothing to show, nothing gained — the sum
result detrimental — offensive — but wait! Diane, we
don't do that — we figure how much in dollars and
cents has been sunk into those little cherubs — we
take this money to a boy I know who can — would love
to — needs to, create one beautiful sculpture to rest
on the clean side of that building — bringing joy —
raising the spirits — the hopes — the taste and
appreciation of who can say how many thousands in
the untold years to come as they walk before this
building? "Look, honey — mediocrity, ugliness doesn't
just happen, it must be created — and takes just as
much time and energy as beauty. But, my god the
difference — the beauty glorifies the city, makes it
live — and the ugliness degrades and kills. You see
now how elementary, how simple for artists to take
their true functional position in society and what
lovely things our cities would be." No, no, of course
it'll never happen. I can hear you yelling out there
now — what about the workmen this one lousy,
disgustingly-talented sculptor threw out of work?
Fuck 'em — I'm not interested in tradesmen or
craftsmen who aren't artists. Yes, of course, a
craftsman can be an artist — and your stinking
unions, which subsidize the incompetent, leveling
all workmen to the same degree of ineptness — why
surpass, why exceed? The drudges, the hangers-on
get the same recognition anyway. Unions aren't
needed by the artist-craftsman — such an asset is he
to any employer, he must be paid comparably good
wages or another, wiser employer, eager for more
profits, will lure him away. O, I don't feel like
going into the union thing now... it's obvious
anyway.

You have walked the jungles toppling idols.
Ripped Atlantis from the sea. Huffed puffed thru

cities. Blew down the walls of cathedrals. Laughed
the sanctified books out. Denounced Christ
Confucius Buddha. Storytellers all, nothing more.
And now. And now you stand to view the havoc you
wrought. And you are alone amidst the rubble and
ashes and thin climbing lines of smoke — All that
remains of doctrine and dogma. And weariness seeps
into your soul. Weariness. Ah, a place to rest, to
lay your head, to lean. But no. Nothing. Chaos. And
your eyes upon agitated churning skies. O God, you
sigh... O God, you cry... And laughter booms hollow
thru the desolation. Yours. Ah, yes, you spat into
the heaven remember? Alone. Alone with the sea the
earth the sun the rain the living the dying. The
spoils. And you know. Yes, now you know. How heavy
knowing... You... You must be God.

Every thinking one, every True intellectual
I've known, finally arrives at the point where he
or she realizes the popularly accepted philosophical
or theological concepts of men are just so much
bullshit: fantastically elaborate rationalizations
built upon rationalization upon rationalization to
the point where digging for its basis or core of
truth if it ever existed, would be ludicrous. All
this is necessary for those who are a part of and
get their security from society as we know it — or
for that matter have ever known it. They must
believe whichever of these gimmicks, being used by
their particular culture, is valid, or reject the
culture; and this is beyond the realm of possibility
for an average mentality. Consider the task... to
question anything and everything — to challenge it
all in the light of truth... impossible, even the
idea would destroy them. They can't even select
their own toothpaste or decide when to use it except
through the influence of a TV personality; so to
challenge the social philosophy that exists as the
nucleus of their society — come now!

But for those few who can and do; for those few insurgent souls who must challenge, must use the keen sharp tool of Mind; for those few who conclude that it's mostly bullshit — what becomes of them? What can happen to them? They must continue to exist in the world they have rejected. Either this or hide, become recluse... but to isolate themselves is impractical... simply because of love... love of and for Human beings. While they may reject the mass of society, they understand the potential of Human love as the great source of gratification. Understanding this, they must live amongst people for the everyday give-and-take of love — in hope of its ecstasy.

And what weird contortions — to be in and out simultaneously... To live in a small corner of society, segregated into their kind, shunning the curious, the un-believers... To move alone through the world, furtively dodging, weaving, looking, listening always for the sweet tone of rapport, and trying to hold themselves aloof — in vain — yes as a salmon holding itself aloof from the sea — hmmm yes, quite cruel... To form a colony, split, flee together, escape, put miles, physical distance — time and space between the lovers and the haters.

But it's all so tiring, so effort-full, so contrived. Wasn't society supposed to let the animal relax in his vigilance towards the carnivorous ones? Yes. And now the hideous cannibal masks of their brothers haunt them... see... they stir restlessly — even in sleep they hunger.

And so for love they stay, continue to suffer the reactionary defensive attitude of the mass, the clannish outright laughter toward every physical, philosophical or esthetic effect of their inherent differentness of Mind. How diabolically insidious the torture inflicted upon them... Books banned, burned or censored... All theater: legitimate, TV,

film — all forced to the level of mass comprehension...
Because of their inevitable non-conformity of speech,
mannerism, dress, not only are they ostracized —
they expect this — but even their physical freedom
is in jeopardy. They, the natural fall-guy for every
social purge, constantly interrogated, persecuted,
imprisoned in the name of every concept or
condition deemed threatening to their particular
culture — whether the crime be called communism,
vagrancy, poverty, homosexuality, cunnilingus,
pornography, atheism, drug abuse... enough enough
enough.

What society is really saying — "Get in line or
get out" and I understand and I can't really blame
them, because these rebels against the commonly-
accepted, keep getting a voice into things and
causing confusion. Perhaps not enough to really
disrupt anything but it can be annoying and it is
annoying and so every time one inopportunely opens
the mouth or writes a thing, or loves an underage
girl or boy, or gets broke, or paints a picture, or
just tries to escape they kick him in the ass and
it's fun or throw him in jail or just ostracize him —
always jolly to have a whipping boy.

Why do they exist? Why are they allowed at
all? Why doesn't the establishment exterminate them
on sight — liquidate them? They've tried; didn't
work. Everything that works, everything of
beauty... they developed, brought into the world...
From the candle to the arc-light... From the oxcart
to the double overhead cam go-machine... From sticks
on a hollow log to Stravinsky: From scratching on a
cave wall to Monet... From melons in a stream to
Electrolux... From Langley to strato-flight liners...
From Plato to Krishnamurti... sure, but they suffer,
have down through the ages. It hurts thinking of

their pain but they won't be destroyed; will be heard in spite of all.

So let's go back to the time when these outcasts first thought and fought their way up out of the morass. What happened on the climb to godhood — where was their tangent?: : :

They usually become egotistically involved with the fact of their difference; identify with the great historical outcasts, embrace the esoteric and sit on their asses. Becoming at best a creative artist, never a creative life. They join small or large groups of forsaken rebels where they sit in small cafés, dingy rooms and penthouses while degenerating mentally and physically with the now static ideals and dope... o yes!!! Always the Dope. Something must replace great warm-breasted mother society, for even the mother of their flesh has turned them away — or in. And the aloneness is overwhelming, un-understandable... and I tell you it's beautiful... Would you get off your ass and begin again to use the incredibly wonderful reasoning power that got you into this mess initially? If you'll believe me it's the way out and up. Look — don't stop, please... Don't fall asleep, please... I needle you, prod you, come alive, come vital, come...

Life so loaded with such good bliss such good pain; so full of fat little wiggly moments and how clean and bright-eyed you must be, how alert to seize them. No dear ones, don't fall asleep — feed your gut with nutrition and feed your mind — with wisdom. Eat, yes feed on life — yes tear off big hunks, chew and digest, assimilate and life becomes you, and you are life and alive... why "coup de grace?"

O fuck the O the H the P......... it's bad for you.

Now is the time to go off writing again.
Johnny reaching out to quick money, hotshot hood,
infant-style scams and... scummy stealing paperbacks
from Pickwicks' bookshop. Shortchanging the banks
with nine dollar and fifty cent — ten dollar
quarter rolls — "I can make ten, twenty bucks a day,
no hassle!" I'm watching him shrivel, and they're
all feeding on each other and they'll all be eaten.
And Diane and Alianne and Lee all barter-whoring,
playing it safe-sanctioned-style. Oh, no, that never
worked or will. And it's death wrapping his last
web for them, his sly, to-their-ear-whispered "Do as
you're told, deny the animal;" and the answer,
always the same "Well, what the hell! Everybody
steals something — I'm no saint!"

And man, I understand: I graduated from
dropping pennies in the nickel-slots of *Hollywood
Citizen News'* stands — to the phenomenally gutty
advancement of straight-lifting them... character...
to swapping tags on "priced as marked" piles of
swimming trunks: $1.95 tag on a $6.95 pair... clever.
And all those drugstore-stolen paperbacks; and
high school nights car-stripping for my hot-chrome
loaded, Christmas-tree, Model A Ford roadster; and
if it was my color and not nailed down — "watch out"
but good-guy like: never from friends — the big
companies, OK "fair game" — Really, did I hate them?

Then one day, great man Wulf philosophizing
on world hate and war and all — so profound "It's
not world hatred or racial hatred; man, it's self-
hatred, the little germ-seed is in each one of the
sick, oppressed millions or it could never manifest
in a group feeling, like a nation's hate is
representative of the hate in its druggists and
bicycle repairmen, and all nations are just like
individuals: lying, conning, conniving, surface
nice-guying each other, opportunistic and 'What's his
is mine, if I can get it' and stealing.........?"

...and calunnnnnnnk, my brain flippity-flops and
another big building (not mental) block falls into
place, and my hairy chin on my hairless chest
rests, while I stupid-stare at my just described
self: war-maker-monger.

And now if finding your $500-billed lost
wallet... you get it back. And I still don't see
DuPonts or Krupps as saintly groups but what's
theirs is theirs, and safe with and from me. And
now I know the fall-out and news headlined child-
gut-spattering wars are not so much my doing; and
eye-to-eye headhigh, I say "Sweet truth, I know I'm
trying to undo it" and it's with an inside cleaner
feeling. And funny how this new integrity kind of
helps support the floppy corners of my verbal
honesty with its: There is no isolated truth, but
all interwoven and twined like lovers' fingers.

Imagine can you — really, it's to laugh — a
primitive yellow nation comprised of non-stealing,
non-lying, non-self-hating, understanding of
emotional and material cause-and-effect laws, and
earned bread tastes better than hype-conned stolen
cake... Imagine being told they should — for their
land or oil or just to practice — machine-gun and
make father and mother son-less, a lot of Abyssinian
blacks who'd never even heard of Democracy. Hell!
They'd laugh the guy right off the balcony, no
matter what his party, his promise — They didn't, but
I can and do, and so can you. Who knows! — one of
you may want to modern-Christ it... and if so, don't
bleed for them — Life and love for them. The last
one made martyr's blood gushing from his nail holes
look like the key to heaven... And the blood pools
are the ending — not the beginning.

And after one soon soft spring rain — people
start glowing-in-the-dark... and how strange in
this brave new mutation, they don't really look like

people, like people anymore... and all the while,
short-shorn and shortsighted men of finance and
state and their vassals of science with eyes glassy
bright, jumping and glee-clapping and witch-
cackling, and all joined hands, dancing ring-
round-rosy round the kettle, while they brew their
last blood-and-nuclear stew — and vapor our next
transmigration... for doomed capped rockets are
slanting tall and black against the surging
frightened night... doomed capped rockets their
fuses primed and ready, ready for the final
eruption, the final brain fire of lunacy... the
final Banzai scream of paranoia, paranoia... and
now we see the lovely blood-red mushrooms poof and
billow the flaming wounded sky and a billion
charred skulls grin victoriously at the illustrious
peace we won, we won, we won... yes, after one soon
soft spring rain peace, peace, peace...

The End

I'll say it again and again—your hope lies not in your culture but in yourself. You don't have time —you're dying too fast to wait for your culture to come alive and a day to live is all you have.

Thousands of years ago and thousands from now there were and will be people who knew and know what's happening — who contemplate their particular cultural environment with sad sardonic mirth — who accept their intellectual isolation seeking rapport on the level of the few. These few creative-lifed ones, and these alone, even begin to approach human potential.

About the Author

Wulf Zendik (1920-1999) was born in El Paso, Texas, and raised on the streets of Los Angeles. He was the direct descendent of renegade Cherokee Chief John Bowles, and could trace his father's German ancestry back to the days of Charlemagne. Wulf came to writing as a poet, at the age of thirty-five. By that time, he had already been a bookie, biplane pilot, hotrod racer, jazz drummer, singer and nightclub owner. He was also twice-married and -divorced, and had tried his hand at factory work and 50's-style tract-home suburbia. Discontent and disillusioned, he had grown desperate for any genuine sense of hope or fulfillment.

Influenced by American writer and expatriate Henry Miller, Wulf dropped out. He left his home in southeast L.A. and moved to Laurel Canyon in Hollywood, the city's one oasis for artists and intellectuals. There, teetering on the brink of his own insanity, he began to write. The process changed him drastically, and in a short time, he became a guru of the Laurel Canyon scene, advising and inspiring the actors, writers and musicians gathered there.

In 1957, Wulf fell in love with a French ballerina who was about to return to her Paris home. Rather than be without her, he followed her, moving to the city's Left Bank, home to the leading figures of the Beat era. Through a junkie-poet lover, Wulf was introduced to many of them, including poets Allen Ginsberg and Gregory Corso, and painter/dancer Vali Myers. He drank and drugged with them, but he also found them frivolous— shallow and out of touch with real people and life itself—and he clashed with them frequently.

Before leaving Los Angeles, Wulf had begun writing his life's story, a free-form burst of prose and poetry which he titled *a Quest Among the Bewildered*. He continued this work in Paris, and by late 1958, had produced a finished manuscript.

Encouraged by those who recognized his talent, he had begun attending a salon for new writers hosted by the well-known diarist Anais Nin. He had also attracted the attention of Somerset Maugham's literary agent. They were deeply moved by *Quest*, but told him that as an unknown author he was unlikely to find someone willing to publish an autobiographical work. They suggested that he try his hand at fiction, and save *Quest* for later.

Wulf took their advice, and shelved the book. On the Mediterranean coast of Spain, he began work on what would become the 900-page novel *Zendik*—the story of a painter in conflict with the dictates of both the art world and society at large. Wulf returned to the U.S. in 1959, and two years later he met Arol, a twenty-three year-old actress and dancer from New York and San Francisco. Fascinated by each other's artistry and integrity, they began a relationship and partnership that would last until Wulf's death in 1999. Their daughter, Fawn, was born in 1976.

Wulf's literary accomplishments also include 1968's *Blackhawk: The Last American Warrior*—the controversial tale of an eco-assassin committed to saving the Earth through any means necessary—as well as three plays, six volumes of poetry and hundreds of dialogs and essays. But his prominence extends far beyond the traditional confines of literature. Well-known throughout the American and international counterculture as a philosopher, musician, essayist and inventor, Wulf has influenced two generations of iconoclasts and idealists. His legacy continues today at Zendik Arts (www.zendik.org), the avant garde artists' culture which was his home and the living embodiment of his benevolent ideals.

to learn more about Wulf Zendik and his legacy, go to www.zendik.org

Books by Wulf Zendik

a Quest Among The Bewildered
These Are The Tears Of A Satyr
Don't Go
Blackhawk: The Last American Warrior
Zendik
The Reality Is This...
Invocation
The Serminars
Firing in the Streets
This is a Statement of Revolution
Cozmic Responsibility
Deathculture Conditioning
Deathculture Deprogramming
Zendika Metaphysics
Dialogs of the Magus
Collected Poems Vol. 1-6